First World War
and Army of Occupation
War Diary
France, Belgium and Germany

24 DIVISION
Divisional Troops
109 Brigade Royal Field Artillery
1 September 1915 - 31 August 1916

WO95/2198/1

The Naval & Military Press Ltd
www.nmarchive.com
Published in association with The National Archives

Published by

The Naval & Military Press Ltd

Unit 10 Ridgewood Industrial Park,
Uckfield, East Sussex,
TN22 5QE England
Tel: +44 (0) 1825 749494

www.naval-military-press.com
www.nmarchive.com

This diary has been reprinted in facsimile from the original. Any imperfections are inevitably reproduced and the quality may fall short of modern type and cartographic standards.

© Crown Copyright
Images reproduced by permission of The National Archives, London, England, 2015.

Contents

Document type	Place/Title	Date From	Date To
Heading	WO95/2198/1 109 Brigade Royal Field Artillery		
Heading	24th Divisional Divl Artillery 109th Brigade R.F.A. Sep 1915-Aug 1916 Broken Up		
Heading	War Diary Headquarters, 109th Brigade. R.F.A. (24th Division) September 1915 Aug 16		
War Diary	Contes	01/09/1915	10/09/1915
War Diary	Hurionville	10/09/1915	11/09/1915
War Diary	Vaudricourt	12/09/1915	12/09/1915
War Diary	Nouex-Les-Mines	12/09/1915	25/09/1915
War Diary	Philosophe	26/09/1915	30/09/1915
Heading	24th D.A.C. Apr. to Vol 3		
Miscellaneous	A Form. Messages And Signals.		
Miscellaneous	Appen 4 War Diary		
Miscellaneous	Ammunition, Supply and Transport Instructions.	25/09/1915	25/09/1915
Miscellaneous	Extract from "Train Loads for New Army Divisions"		
Heading	Appendix 1 In War Diary		
Miscellaneous			
Miscellaneous	Memorandum		
Miscellaneous			
Miscellaneous	Ammun. Refilling Point.	24/09/1915	24/09/1915
Miscellaneous	March Table	24/09/1915	24/09/1915
Heading	24th Division 109th Bde. R.F.A. Vol 2 Oct. 15		
War Diary	Philosophe	01/10/1915	01/10/1915
War Diary	Guarbecque	02/10/1915	02/10/1915
War Diary	Wallon-Capelle	03/10/1915	03/10/1915
War Diary	Harringhe	04/10/1915	07/10/1915
War Diary	Watou	08/10/1915	08/10/1915
War Diary	Reninghelst	09/10/1915	29/10/1915
Heading	24th Division 109th Bde. R.F.A. Vol. 3 Nov 15		
War Diary	Reninghelst	30/10/1915	25/11/1915
War Diary	Steenvorde	26/11/1915	27/11/1915
War Diary	Nortbecourt	28/11/1915	30/11/1915
Miscellaneous	R.T.O Abeele	01/11/1915	01/11/1915
Miscellaneous			
Miscellaneous	A Form Messages And Signals.		
Miscellaneous	App. 13		
Miscellaneous	C Form (Original). Messages And Signals.		
Heading	24th Div 109th Bde. R.F.A. Vol. 4		
War Diary	Nortbecourt	01/12/1915	04/12/1915
War Diary	Audenfort	05/12/1915	31/12/1915
Heading	109th Bde. R.F.A. Vol. 5		
War Diary	Audenfort	01/01/1916	01/01/1916
War Diary	Buysschuere	02/01/1916	02/01/1916
War Diary	Steenvoorde	03/01/1916	04/01/1916
War Diary	Tering Line	05/01/1916	18/01/1916
War Diary	Poperinghe	18/01/1916	30/01/1916
War Diary	Tering Line	31/01/1916	31/01/1916
Heading	109th Bde R.F.A. Vol. 6		
War Diary	Tering Line	01/02/1916	16/02/1916
War Diary	Poperinghe	17/02/1916	29/02/1916

Heading	109 R.F.A. Vol 7		
War Diary	Poperinghe	01/03/1916	03/03/1916
War Diary	Tering Line	04/03/1916	14/03/1916
War Diary	In The Fields	15/03/1916	18/03/1916
War Diary	Steenvorde	19/03/1916	31/03/1916
War Diary	Tering Line	01/04/1916	30/04/1916
Miscellaneous	The Officer i/c Adjutant Generals Office Base. Herewith Vol. 10 of War Diary.		
War Diary	T 23bs	01/05/1916	31/05/1916
Miscellaneous	O i/c A.G's Office Base. Herewith War Diary For June 1916		
War Diary	T23. C.4.2	01/06/1916	05/07/1916
War Diary	M 18 C.5.2	06/07/1916	21/07/1916
War Diary	Q 32.b.5.6	22/07/1916	26/07/1916
War Diary	Crouy	27/07/1916	30/07/1916
War Diary	Daours	31/07/1916	31/07/1916
Heading	24th Divisional Artillery 109th Brigade Royal Field Artillery August 1916		
Miscellaneous	Secret. Headquarters, 24th Divisional Artillery. Herewith Vol 12 of War Diary. 6.9.16		
War Diary	Daours	01/08/1916	03/08/1916
War Diary	Bois Des Tailles	04/08/1916	11/08/1916
War Diary	A.15.C.4.5	12/08/1916	26/08/1916
War Diary	S.22.C.9.2	27/08/1916	31/08/1916
Miscellaneous	Appendix 1	13/08/1916	13/08/1916
Miscellaneous	Os C. Batteries.	15/08/1916	15/08/1916
Miscellaneous	Programme For Shoot	15/08/1916	15/08/1916
Miscellaneous	106th F.A.B.	16/08/1916	16/08/1916
Miscellaneous	Os. C. Batteries.	17/08/1916	17/08/1916
Miscellaneous	Os. C. Batteries.	28/08/1916	28/08/1916
Miscellaneous	D C. Battery	28/08/1916	28/08/1916
Miscellaneous	D.C. Batteries	29/08/1916	29/08/1916

WO/95/2198/1

109 Brigade Royal Field Artillery

24TH DIVISION
DIVL ARTILLERY

109TH BRIGADE R.F.A.

SEP 1915 - AUG 1916

Broken up

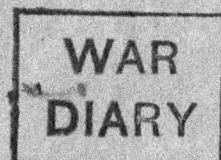

Headquarters,

109th BRIGADE, R.F.A.

(24th Division)

S E P T E M B E R

1 9 1 5

1

Aug 16

Army Form C.2118

WAR DIARY
or
INTELLIGENCE SUMMARY.
(Erase heading not required.)

Instructions regarding War Diaries and Intelligence Summaries are contained in F. S. Regs., Part II. and the Staff Manual respectively. Title pages will be prepared in manuscript.

SEPTEMBER

Place	Date	Hour	Summary of Events and Information	Remarks and references to Appendices
Conties	1st Sept 1915		Delivered at Conties 11.30 a.m. having arrived at Havre from England on the 31st Aug 1915. The Brigade moved into a field near Conties where the horses & guns were picketed & parked. Officers and men billeted in houses & barns. Wet weather.	
Conties	2nd		Very heavy rain during which the brigade was settling down in camp & billets.	
"	3rd		Too wet for drill, but specialist were exercised. Horses were exercised on the roads.	
"	4th		Usual routine drill &c. Weather very troublesome.	
"	5th		Sunday. Church parade at noon. The Brigade Ammn. column went for a route march.	
"	6th		Brigade route march. OC & BC's attended HQ at Beauvainville & be introduced to GOC I Corps. Country round ST DENO U 12 reconnoitred by Adjutant with the Brigade Major with a view to next days field day.	

ARRAS Map Sheet 7. H. Mackay Lt R.7a

WAR DIARY
or
INTELLIGENCE SUMMARY.

(Erase heading not required.)

Army Form C. 2118

Place	Date	Hour	Summary of Events and Information	Remarks and references to Appendices
CONTES	7th Sept. 16		Genl. Field Reynolds G.O.C. 2nd Cdn. Div. Brigade occupied position chosen on the previous day and relieved to Camp about 2.30 pm.	
"	8th	"	Received orders the ready to move on the following day, the brigade spent the day preparing for move. Packing Vehicles etc.	
"	9th	"	Brigade received orders & moved off at 9.30 am. On arrival at SAVY & arrested the van to halt for horses, & moved on to FLECHIN another 1½ miles, where we bivouced for the night. There were no casualties, owing to the fine weather & good état of the roads, men horses were wonderfully little depressed. The Supply & Baggage sections of the Divisional Train completely broke down and no Rations or forage arrived.	
"	10th	"	The move off of the brigade was very much delayed owing to the non arrival of rations & forage which should have arrived on the previous evening. It eventually arrived at 8.30 am the Brigade moving off at 9 am late. There it took place after having a hurried meal. B & D battalion with left half of B Col. clear to join 1st Corps at CHOCQUES.	Arras of sheet 7

Arras of sheet 7.

WAR DIARY
or
INTELLIGENCE SUMMARY.
(Erase heading not required.)

Army Form C. 2118

Place	Date	Hour	Summary of Events and Information	Remarks and references to Appendices
HURIONVILLE	10th Sept	Cont^d	and left in advance of the remainder of the brigade. C & D batteries with half of the B.A. Column 107th Brigade then joined the 109th Brigade to march with us and the temporary attachment. The brigade bivouacked at HURIONVILLE but the carts had difficulty, about 10 occurred soon after arrival evening. Two men were hurt on the march but their injuries were slight. A Court Martial was held on Bt Cpl S B Cochrane who was reduced to the ranks, the sentence being confirmed that day.	
"	11th		The brigade moved off at 9.30 am, being again delayed by the non-arrival of rations forage, the horses were beginning to show the effects of this irregular feeding. O.C. A Battery & B.C. of his battery of the 107 Brigade went on by motor car to reconnoitre position for G.O.C. R.A. & Groups and returned to the brigade which had arrived at HACHIN and the remainder of the brigade were ordered at VAUDRICOURT, the Brigade headquarters going into billets at NOEUX-LES-MINES.	
VAUDRICOURT	12th		C battery moved into Gun pits at MAROC GARDENS near LES-BREBIS. During this began their limbers & wagon lines. A battery took over Gun Pits. Bethune continued sheet.	

WAR DIARY
or
INTELLIGENCE SUMMARY

Army Form C.2118

Place	Date	Hour	Summary of Events and Information	Remarks and references to Appendices
NOEUX-LES-MINES	12	6	Carhed been prepared at PHILOSOPHE near VERMELLES. C.D. Battn 107th Brigade went to gain their various groups their wagon remains at the original wagon line.	
	13	6	A & C batteries Hq Gr and C.D. 107th spent the day in completing their Gun pits and registering targets in areas allotted to them. A/109 was placed for tactical purposes in a Group commanded by Lt Col H.B. Hunter R.F.A. C M G and C/109 in Group commanded by Lt Col Sharpe R.F.A. 8 alarm was ordered for 108 rounds per gun to the dumps in Gun pits.	
	14	6	Registering completed, ammunition dug out to the detachment continued, ammunition being sent up by night per wagon lines.	
	15	6	In the evening a portion of the D.A.C. arrived from near Montreuil C Battery was the subject of an attack during the night and four rounds landed in the immediate vicinity of its gun pits. One round fell into the room occupied by 2/Lt Palmer and 2/Lt McAlister, fragments passing through Bethune combined sheet	

WAR DIARY
or
INTELLIGENCE SUMMARY.

(Erase heading not required.)

Army Form C.

Place	Date	Hour	Summary of Events and Information	Remarks and references to Appendices
NOEUX-LES-MINES.	15th	Cont.d	through the floor into the room in which were Major L.S.D. Craven and 2/Lt Aldrich. No serious damage was done to any of these officers except a few minor injuries. A new home had to be found as their present was badly damaged.	
	16th		A & C Batteries were improving their Gun pits and Dug outs.	
	17th		Nothing of importance occurred.	
	18th		Normal conditions obtained, only retaliations going on.	
	19th		A & C Batteries completing their dumps of Ammunition; orders having been received authorising the exchange of shrapnel for lyddite, 108 rounds per gun were dumped and the first line wagons kept full.	
	20th		Col Butcher H.Y., 108th Brigade R.F.A. whose Headquarters were in the vicinity of MAROC GARDENS, was killed by H.E. shell, while covering to rescue some	

Army Form C. 2118

WAR DIARY
or
INTELLIGENCE SUMMARY.
(Erase heading not required.)

Instructions regarding War Diaries and Intelligence Summaries are contained in F. S. Regs., Part II. and the Staff Manual respectively. Title pages will be prepared in manuscript.

Place	Date	Hour	Summary of Events and Information	Remarks and references to Appendices
NOEUX-LES-MINES	20th (Cont.d)		civilians who had been hit.	
	21st		Preliminary bombardment commenced at 6.0.a.m. A & C Batteries were allowed 80 rounds per gun daily for their task.	
	22nd		Continuation of bombardment. Guns giving good results.	
	23rd		O.O. visited B & D Batteries, attached to the 1st Corps and found them carrying out practically the same programme. The enemy were not expending much ammunition in reply, but a few 5.9 and 4.2 shells were falling near B & D Batteries just N. of VERMELLES who seemed to attract the greater part of the enemy's fire at this time. Tube pattern helmets were issued to all ranks.	
	24th		Orders were received for move of wagon lines of A/109 and C & D Batteries 107th Brigade. Bombardment continued.	

WAR DIARY
or
INTELLIGENCE SUMMARY.
(Erase heading not required.)

Place	Date	Hour	Summary of Events and Information	Remarks and references to Appendices
NOEUX-LES-MINES	25th		During the night 24/25th the wagons of A. Battery, remainder of C Battery along with the wagons of C + D Batteries 107th Brigade moved from VAUDRICOURT to NOEUX-LES-MINES. The two half B.A Columns of 107th + 109th Brigades moved at 1 a.m on 25th. At 7 p.m O.C received orders through A/109 to report to C.R.A 24th Division immediately at VERMELLES and proceeded as foot as possible considering the congestion of the roads, newly made tracks being impossible owing to their greasiness. Arrived about 9.30 p.m. and received orders to collect "A" + "C" Batteries from the groups to which they had been attached and bring them up to the neighbourhood of PHILOSOPHE. A. Battery wagon line moved to PHILOSOPHE. A. Battery wagon line arrived at about 5.0 a.m the guns remaining ~~with others~~ in position.	
PHILOSOPHE	26th		Arrived with Head Quarters Staff + half B.A.C at field W. of PHILOSOPHE about 5.0 a.m and tried to get into touch with C Battery unsuccessfully. About 6.30 a.m reported to Head Quarters R.A. and found that B + D Batteries had been sent forward by the G.O.C, R.A. Orders were received to hold A + C Batteries in	

WAR DIARY
or
INTELLIGENCE SUMMARY.

Place	Date	Hour	Summary of Events and Information	Remarks and references to Appendices
PHILOSOPHE	26th (Cont.)		reserve, the latter only arriving about 10.0. a.m. B and D Batteries were placed in a group under Lt. Col. COATES, Commanding 107th Brigade R.F.A. and worked under his orders, A. Battery remaining in action in its old position, having been ordered back into the gun-pits by Lt-Col. ELTON Commanding R.A. 1st Div. whose Head Quarters were in that locality. I was in touch with the G.O.C., R.A. all day. D Battery had been pushed well forward but owing to a mis-understanding its ammunition supply failed and pending more rounds being sent up the detachments were temporarily withdrawn. They went up again later and the guns were taken back to a position in rear by order of the G.O.C., R.A. B. Battery remaining in action all day & night.	
	27th.	About 9. a.m.	I received orders from G.O.C., R.A. to send A & C Batteries to Lt. Col. COATES' group and to get into touch with 13th Gen. WARDROP Commanding R.A., Guards Division at LA ROUTOIRE. My Brigade was to remain under command of Lt. Col. COATES. I told him the orders I had received and that I had ordered O.C's A & C Batteries to get into touch with him and	

Place	Date	Hour	Summary of Events and Information	Remarks and references to Appendices
PHILOSOPHE	27th (Contd.)		take his orders. Br. Genl. WARDROP. was not at LA ROUTOIRE. I then went to Hd Qrs 21st Div where I had been told he could be found. Br. Genl. ALEXANDER said he was expected there at 1.0 o'clock. As he had not arrived by 2.30 p.m. I went to SAILLY-LA-BOURSE in the hope of finding him. I saw Br. Genl. CAREY and Br. Genl. THOMAS neither of whom could direct me to him. On my return I visited B+D Batteries, but as an action was going on at the time I thought it unwise to obtrude myself on Br. Genl. WARDROP. The night passed quietly. As far as I could gather A + C Batteries had received orders from Lt. Col. COATES to remain where they were and they did not seem to be doing very much.	
	28th		Hd Qrs in PHILOSOPHE with wagon lines + B.A.C. in the vicinity. B+D Batteries were in action about 1000 yards S.E. of LA ROUTOIRE FARM and during the day were firing on houses in BENEFONTAINE. A + C Batteries were in action in PHILOSOPHE just west of railway having an observing station on FOSSE 3. Their objective in the morning was the same as that of B + D and later hostile batteries S. of BENEFONTAINE. The group under Lt. Col. COATES	

Place	Date	Hour	Summary of Events and Information	Remarks and references to Appendices
PHILOSOPHE	28th	(cont.d)	was attached to the Guards Division. At 3.45 p.m all Batteries bombarded, preparatory to an advance by Guards Division. There was little firing from the R.A. during the night, 109th Brigade not firing at all. There was heavy rain during the night. The supply of rations was again deficient.	
	29th		At 9.0.a.m orders were received from G.O.C, R.A 24th. Division to vacate positions by sections, after dark on the 29/30 and 30/1. The positions to be occupied by 61st. Brigade. The Hd.Qs of Brigade and Batteries to be relieved on the second night. Orders were given accordingly but about 8.0 p.m orders were received through the Group Commander at LA ROUTOIRE that B & D Batteries were to remain where they were and only the sections of A & C Batteries were to be relieved. The Guns, however, of the 61st. Batteries detailed to relieve B & D Batteries came up late in the evening and had to go back again. B Battery was very heavily shelled during the afternoon and the gunners had to take cover as the guns were in a very exposed position and were being enfiladed from the direction of FOSSE 8. The wagon lines of	

WAR DIARY
or
INTELLIGENCE SUMMARY.
(Erase heading not required.)

Army Form C. 2118.

Place	Date	Hour	Summary of Events and Information	Remarks and references to Appendices
PHILOSOPHE	29th (cont)		B & D Batteries moved to a position W. of PHILOSOPHE in the same field with C Battery and B.A.C.	
	30th		Heavy firing all day. Capt. Hart and Lieut Hogge went to the forward station in the front Infantry trench and while on their way were heavily shelled. Their guide, a Sergeant in K.R.R. was killed and Lt. HOGGE was wounded in the knee. Capt. Hart managed to get him to advanced Dressing Station in LOOS. A & D Batteries withdrew after dark to their wagon lines in PHILOSOPHE	

H Robertson Lt.
Adjutant, 109th Brigade, R.F.A.

File 6 Vol 3

121/7931

War diary app 4

"A" Form.
MESSAGES AND SIGNALS.
Army Form C. 2121.

TO: 24th Dwn Amtn Col.

Sender's Number: BM 58
Day of Month: 30/9/15
AAA

Orders received from 11th Corps
Reference ARRAS map 7
The following wagons of 24th D.A.C. will march today 20th starting 8.45 am aaa

(1.) Half wagons carrying 18 pr Amtn for 106 Brigade to 2nd D.A.C. at OBLINGHEM about 1½ miles N.W. of BETHUNE, and half to 7th D.A.C. at FOUQUIERES LEZ BETHUNE 1½ miles SW of BETHUNE aaa

All wagons carrying 18 pr Amtn for 108 Brigade to 47th DAC at LABUSSIERE 5 miles S.W. of BETHUNE aaa

(2) Waggons will march together to WESTREHEM aaa

"A" Form.
Army Form C. 2121.
MESSAGES AND SIGNALS.

TO { 24th Div Amtn Column

AAA

(3) Halt 1st night at CREQUY (via BEAURAINVILLE and ROYON) Halt 2nd night at WESTREHEM (via FRUGES and LAIRES) Arrive destinations 22nd.

(4) Rations will be given you up to and for 22nd.

(5) Remainder of D.A.C. will march to BEAURAINVILLE there to be billetted.

(6) Your group commander has been informed.

(7) Please acknowledge.

From BM 24th Div Art
Time 12.30 AM

Appen 4. War Diary 24th D.A.C.
Appen. No.

Statement of Personel, animals,
Vehicles: allotted at BEAURAIN
VILLE. Sept 20th 1915.

Head Qrs as per War Estabm't
No. 1. Section. S.A.A. pmp.

1 Officer (Tempr 2. Lt Garnett Clarke)
1 Sergt. 73 other ranks.
  93 horses and mules.
  14 Wagons.

No. 3 Section:-

1 Officers. T. 2-Lt E. Sanders.
1 B.S.M. 1 Sergt. 66 other ranks.
  81 horses and mules.
  12 Wagons.

14 horses received 21.9.15 at
BOURAINVILLE
distributed 8 to No 1 Sec
            6 to No 3 Sec

24 Dec.

For retention DWR
25.9.15

Copy No......... 5

Ammunition, Supply and Transport Instructions.

When an advance is ordered from the Concentration Area, which is occupied on the night of the 24/25th. the following Transport will accompany the Troops :-
Per Battalion.

Water Cart.	1.
Wagons Limbered G.S. for S.A.A.	5.
" " " " Tools.	2.
" " for Machine Guns.	2.
" " " " S.A.A.	2.
Pack Mules.	8.
Cart Maltese for Medical	1.
Bomb Wagon.	1.

All this Transport will be under the command of Battalion Transport Officers, and such portions of it as Divisional Commanders decide will be brigaded in rear of each Brigade.

2. The remainder of the Transport will be parked (off the roAD). Head of the Column for 24th. Division on the road BEUVRY-BETHUNE, West and clear of the town of BEUVRY.

Head of the Column for 21st. Division on the road, NOEUX LES MINES - PLACE A BRUAY, West and clear of the town NOEUX LES MINES.

The Transport of the Guards Division (less what accompanies the Troops) will form up in rear of the 21st or 24th. Divisional Trains, according to whichever road the Guards Division advances.

Other Transport will be formed up in the following order :-
(a) Remainder of 1st. Line Transport :-
Per Battalion.
Water Cart.   1.
Officers' Mess.   1.
Travelling Kitchens. 4.

(b) Supply Sections in order of Brigades and Divisional Troops as they have advanced.

(c) Baggage Sections in order of Brigades and Divisional Troops as they have advanced.

When an advance of the Transport is ordered (a) and (b) will go forward under the Command of the Officers Commanding Brigade Companies of the Train. The Brigade Supply Officer will accompany (a) and (b) O.C. Train will remain with (c).

Supply wagons of Divisional Troops will be attached to Brigade Companies of the Train under Divisional arrangements.

3. SUPPLY.

Railheads until further orders.	LILLERS.
Refilling Points.	24th. Division in BETHUNE at the Marche aux Chevaux on the road leading to the canal.
	21st. Division HALLICOURT.
	Guards Division to be selected by Guards Division.
Ammunition Railhead.	ST. VENANT.

EXTRACT FROM "TRAIN LOADS FOR NEW ARMY DIVISIONS"

(WAR ESTABLISHMENTS, PART VII., NEW ARMIES, ISSUED WITH A.O. of 1st AUGUST 1915)

UNIT	OFFICERS	OTHERS	Horses: OFFICERS	Horses: OTHERS	GUNS	Vehicles: 4-WHEEL	Vehicles: 2-WHEEL	BICYCLES	STORES	COMPARTMENTS	HORSE BOXES	CATTLE TRUCKS	VEHICLE TRUCKS	VANS	TOTAL RAILWAY VEHICLES	NUMBER OF TRAINS REQUIRED
1 Dvl. Ammn. Col.	2	69	:	88	:	14	,	-	,	10	=	12	14	2	30	1
=	2	69	:	88	:	13 ¹⁴	,	-	,	10	=	12	13 ¹⁴	2	29 ³⁰	1
=	2	69	:	88	:	13 ¹⁴	,	-	,	10	=	12	13 ¹⁴	2	29 ³⁰	1
=	2	69	:	88	:	13	:	-	,	10	=	12	13	2	29	1
=	-	69	:	88	:	13	-	-	,	10	=	12	13	2	29	1
=	-	68	:	88	:	13	-	,	,	10	=	12	14	2	30	1
=	-	68	:	88	:	13	-	,	,	10	=	12	14	2	30	1
=	-	68	:	89	:	13	-	,	,	10	=	12	14	2	30	1

{ 8 }

549 / 555
703 / 715
107

Wilson Bumby
Lieut. R.F.A.
O/Adjt. 24th Dvl. Ammn. Column.

Deepcut.
27.8.1915

Appendix I
for Windsor

Train lands from FARNBOROUGH
L.S.W.R. Sept 1st 1915
2nd R.A Divisional office

TRAIN	Sex	4 wheel vehicle	2 wheel veh.	Bic.	Off.	N.Orman	Horse d.	Horses	Horses O.	Horses R.	Horses (draw)
1st	I	14		1	1	69	84	1		3	
2nd	I	14			1	69	84	1		5	
3rd	I	7 2.two horse		1	1	40	34	1		2	18
4th	II	7 2.two horse		1	1	29	34	1			
5th	II	13		1	1	69	78	1		5	6
6th	II	13		1	1	69	78	1		5	6
	II					5					6
	III	13 1 twd horse		1	1	64	74	1		2	4
Hops	III		1		1	1	2	1			
7th	III	13		1	1	69	78	1		6	
Hops	III		1		≠	1	2	≠		1	
	III	7 1two horse	≠	1	1	40	38	1		2	14
8th	Hops	6	1	1	2	30	25	3		6 76	
						555	611	13		37	54

W. P. Griffith & Sons Ltd., Printers, Old Bailey, E.C.
[326] W9668/1672 2500m 12/14s **75 78**   Forms C. 348/61

No. _____

MEMORANDUM.

Army Form C. 348.

From

From

To

To

ANSWER.

_____ 191

_____ 191

No. 1 Section

For No. 1 train. parade at 12mn / 1 am. Sept 1st — train leaves 4. am
" 2 train parade at 1am / 2am " — 5. 10 am.
" 3 " " " 2 / 3 am " — 6. 10 am

3 # Men absent from No 1.

No 3

For No 6 train parade at 5.50 / 6.50 am. — train leaves 9. 50 am
" 7 " parade at 6 / 7.50. — train leaves 10. 50 am
" 8 " parade at 7 / 8.50. — train " 11.50 am

No 2 Section

No. 3 train parade at parade 2 / 3 am. — train leaves. 6. 10
No. 4 train parade at parade 3.50 / 4.50 am — " 7. 50
No. 5 train parade at 4 / 5.45. — " 8. 45
" 6th " " " 5 / 6.50 am — " 9. 50

<u>Ammun. Refilling Point.</u>	24th. Division at cross roads south of OBLINGHEM. 21st. Division on the road HESDIGNEUL to LA-BOISSIERE. At Ammunition Refilling Point.
<u>Position of D.A.C.</u> <u>Position of Sub-Parks.</u> <u>Position of Supply Column.</u> <u>Communications.</u>	At Ammunition Railhead. At Supply Railhead. All Supply Columns and Sub-Parks will detail one Motor Cyclist to be at the head of the baggage column of the Division they are supplying at BEUVRY and NOEUX LES MINES.
<u>Roads to be followed.</u>	As by Traffic Map issued to all concerned.
<u>Rum.</u>	Will be issued for consumption on the night of 25th. and 26th.
<u>Extra Issues.</u>	Extra Rations of cheese and Pea Soup will be issued on 24th. to supplement the Iron Ration and must be carried under Divisional arrangements.

24th. Sept. 1915.   Sd. R. FORD. Br. Genl.
H.Q. 11th. Corps.   D.A.&Q.M.G. 11th. Corps.

SECRET.   11th. Corps. No. C/43.

Headquarters,
       24th. Division.

     Herewith Ammunition, Supply and Transport instructions in connection with the march forward.

H.Q. 11th. Corps.   Sd. R. FORD. Br. Genl.
24th. Sept. 1915.   D.A.&Q.M.G. 11th. Corps.

....

....

              Forwarded for your information.

In the Field,   Colonel.
24. 9. 15.   A.A.&Q.M.G. 24th. Division.

MARCH TABLE 24.9.15.

Unit.	Starting Point.	Time.	Route. Vide Map 1/100,000 HAZEBROUCK Sheet.	Destination Vide Sqd.Map 1/40,000 Sht.36.B.	Remarks.
A Sqn.Q.O.R.G.Yeo.	Road Junc. just B in BUSNES	6.12 p.m.	C in CHAU - Rd.junc.at last E in L'ECLEME - road junc.St M in GONNEHEM - CHOCQUES - road junc.E of railway crossing S of V in VENDIN LEZ BETHUNE - thence by road running S.W. and STA.(S.of BETHUNE) - thence road running N.W.to main BETHUNE - BEUVRY road to Y in BEUVRY.	ANNEZIN	Not to cross the LILLERS - L'ECLEME road before 6.45 p.m.
Div.H.Q.	ditto.	6.15 p.m.	ditto	BETHUNE Square E.11.a.	
73rd Inf.Bde. 129th Fd.Coy.R.E.	ditto.	6.18 p.m.	ditto	Head to crossroads at Y of BEUVRY. Tail about branch Rly.line in Square E.18.	No village.enter BEUVRY village. On piqueting from road the Div.Cyclist Coy. will join 73rd Bde. Ars.
72nd Inf.Bde. 104th Fd.Coy.R.E.	Crossroads at 1st L of LA PIERRIERE.	6.45 p.m.	ditto	In rear of 73rd Inf.Bde. Tail in BETHUNE.	
71st Inf.Bde. 103rd Fd.Coy.R.E. 12th Sher.Foresters.	Road junc.S. of M in LA MICUSILERIE	7.45 p.m.	BUSNES - Follow in rear of 72nd Inf.Bde.	BETHUNE (S.& S.W.end) (STA.excluded).	
74th Fd.Amb.	ditto	7.45 p.m.	ditto.	CHAMP DE MARS BETHUNE.	
73rd Fd.Amb. 41st Sanitary Sec. M.T.Workshop A.S.C.	Crossroads at last L of LA PIERRIERE.	8.45 p.m.	ditto.	ditto.	Route from Rly.Crossing N.W.of BETHUNE is the main road to BETHUNE.
72nd Fd.Amb.	ditto.	8.45 p.m.	ditto.	ditto.	
S.A.A.Sections of 105th,107th,108th Bdes.R.F.A.	South of B in BOURECQ on LILLERS-rd.	7.45 p.m.	LILLERS - L'ECLEME thence as above.	ANNEZIN (North end).	
Remainder of D.A.C.	ditto.		To follow S.A.A.Sects.to N of GONNEHEM thence by 2nd N in LAMBUZO tp OBLINGHEM.	Crossroads S. of OBLINGHEM. Ref.1/100,000 Map.	

121/7608

24th Division

169th Bde: R.F.a.
Vol 2
Oct. 15

Army Form C. 2118

109th Brigade, R.F.A.

WAR DIARY
or
INTELLIGENCE SUMMARY.
(Erase heading not required.)

Instructions regarding War Diaries and Intelligence Summaries are contained in F. S. Regs., Part II. and the Staff Manual respectively. Title pages will be prepared in manuscript.

Place	Date	Hour	Summary of Events and Information	Remarks and references to Appendices
Philosophe	Oct 1st		The Brigade being now re-assembled in Philosophe, under Col CRAIG, moved at 5.30 A.M. to the northward, their first orders being to send on an officer to report at BERGUETTE. The Brigade billeted for the night at GUARBECQUE	
GUARBECQUE	Oct 2nd		Brigade moved off at 9 A.M. and marched in rear of 106th Brigade R.F.A to WALLON-CAPELLE when they were billeted for the night.	
WALLON-CAPELLE	Oct 3rd		Brigade moved off crossing the railway at 7.45 A.M. and marched on leaving CASSEL to the left, via STEINWORDE to HARRINGHE, where they were billeted, the horses being in fields and the men in barns and tents	
HARRINGHE	Oct 4th		Spent the day in cleaning up.	
	Oct 5th		Cleaning up and drawing stores	

2353 Wt. W3544/1454 700,000 5/15 D. D. & L. A.D.S.S./Forms/C. 2118.

Army Form C. 211

109th Brigade, R.F.A.

WAR DIARY
or
INTELLIGENCE SUMMARY.

(Erase heading not required.)

Instructions regarding War Diaries and Intelligence Summaries are contained in F. S. Regs., Part II. and the Staff Manual respectively. Title pages will be prepared in manuscript.

Place	Date	Hour	Summary of Events and Information	Remarks and references to Appendices
HARRINGHE	Oct 6th		Drill order for inspection by Maj.Gen. CAPPER commanding 24th Div. He was accompanied by Brig.Gen.Sir G.Thomas commanding 24th Div Artillery and Col.C.Stewart G.S.O.1 Twenty one L.D horses arrived	
	Oct 7th		Commanding Officer and 2 officers per Battery and 1 from B.A.C with sufficient of Head Quarters and Battery Staffs to make up a party of 60 all ranks proceeded to the Ypres Salient to be attached to 53rd Brigade R.F.A. The remainder of Brigade were detailed for a route march from their billets to WATOU and on the march were inspected by Lieut.Gen. PLUMER commanding 2nd Army and his Army & Div'l Staff.	
WATOU	Oct 8th		The Brigade less party above mentioned, marched to RENINGHELST and were billeted there.	

WAR DIARY
or
INTELLIGENCE SUMMARY.

Army Form C. 2118

109th Brigade, R.F.A.

Place	Date	Hour	Summary of Events and Information	Remarks and references to Appendices
RENINGHELST	Oct 9th		The party from 53rd Bde R.F.A which on previous day had inspected gun-pits etc. of that Brigade, returned to the Head-Quarters of the Brigade. The positions of the various batteries were – "A" and "B" batteries in wood of Yser and "C" and "D" on East. The Batteries spent the day in trying to make themselves comfortable. The B.A.G. were accommodated in a field North of BOESCHEPPE.	
	Oct 10th		Batteries still trying to prepare as far as possible wagon lines for the winter, as now the Brigade remains in this area. The Head Quarters was fixed in a farm in the centre of RENINGHELST. Some stoves and clothing and two water carts were received from Ordnance Stores.	

WAR DIARY or INTELLIGENCE SUMMARY

109th Brigade, R.F.A.

Army Form C. 2118

Place	Date	Hour	Summary of Events and Information	Remarks and references to Appendices
RENINGHELST	Oct 11th		Repairing huts and stables for which. Drills being carried on and Specialists Trained	
	Oct 12th		As on Monday, back office work being attended to	
	Oct 13th		Orders having been received that to some extent it was likely that the Brigade would take over the positions occupied by the 53rd How'r Brigade R.F.A. reconnoitred those positions and got in touch with the batteries to be relieved obtaining all available information with regard to registration etc. O.C. adjutant went to the Brigade Head Quarters of the 53rd Bde for the same purpose.	
	Oct 14th		O.C went with G.O.C. R.A to visit H.Q. of the 51st Brigade R.F.A and also the Belgian H.Q. R.arty. Routine drill being carried on by all batteries.	

War Diary, 109th Brigade, R.F.A. — Intelligence Summary

Army Form C. 2118

Place	Date	Hour	Summary of Events and Information	Remarks and references to Appendices
RENINGHELST	6.6.15		O.C. inspected wagon lines of C & D batteries during the morning.	
"	6.6.16		Major W.E. Graves 9/109 went on short leave owing to serious illness of his father. Capt B/109 accompanied the Brigade Major to make a reconnaissance in the neighbourhood of VOORMEZEELE with a view to finding a forward position for his battery. Orders were received for A & B batteries to relieve C & D batteries 53rd Howr. Brigade a section of the 1st time, first section moving up on Sunday 17th after dark, and the remaining section & headquarters on the 18th. O.C.'s adjutant & O.C.'s these batteries were engaged in making necessary arrangements.	
"	6.6.17		Divine Service for all batteries. Capt Hart accompanied by Mr Milton continued his reconnaissances; his report being sent to G.O.C. R.A. cont—	

… Army Form C. 2118

100th Brigade, R.F.A.

WAR DIARY
INTELLIGENCE SUMMARY.

(Erase heading not required.)

Place	Date	Hour	Summary of Events and Information	Remarks and references to Appendices
RENINGHELST	Oct 17		cont One section D battery moved into its position near LAKE of DICKEBUSCH, relieving similar section of D/53rd brigade. One section A/109 moved up to relieve a section of C/53rd brigade but on arrival found this arrangement counter ordered. The guns and wagons were parked in the vicinity, the men being accommodated in the 53rd dug outs. They then awaited further orders sending horses back to wagon lines. Rations drawn in bulk by Brigade and re-distributed	
RENINGHELST	Oct 18		One section of A/109 moved by orders of 5th Corps into position which had been occupied by C/53rd brigade. Remainder section of D/109 Headquarters of that battery relieved the remainder section of D/53rd brigade. The country in the neighbourhood was reconnoitred for positions for B+C batteries.	

Army Form C. 2118

106th Brigade, R.F.A.

WAR DIARY
or
INTELLIGENCE SUMMARY.
(Erase heading not required.)

Place	Date	Hour	Summary of Events and Information	Remarks and references to Appendices
RENINGHELST	Oct 10		D/106 registered two points in enemy's trenches and was called upon to fire 16 rounds as reprisal. C/106 completed taking over its positions from B/53rd Brigade. The B.A.C. moved from BOESINGHE to a position N.E. of RENINGHELST in the same field as C/106 wagon line.	
	Oct 11 0230		C/106 registered its zero line and a portion of first line hostile trench.	
	Oct 11		Position for C/106 was finally approved and C/106 went up at night to commence making gun-pits. All batteries sent wagons to YPRES to obtain material for making huts and stables.	
	Oct 12		O.C. went to inspect position N of VOORMEZEELE for two guns of B/106 and it was settled that although not nearly [...]	

2353 Wt. W2544/1454 700,000 5/15 D. D. & L.   A.D.S.S./Forms/C. 2118.

108th Brigade, R.F.A.

WAR DIARY or INTELLIGENCE SUMMARY

Place	Date	Hour	Summary of Events and Information	Remarks and references to Appendices
RENINGHELST	Oct 22		cont:- desirable positions; gun pits should be made there with a view to being occupied if a special task was required of the Brigade necessitating guns being well forward. The intention was that Cage Pits should never be occupied by men or guns except when the actual task necessitated. Lecture by MAJOR SIR J. KEANE. R.A. on trench mortars.	
"	Oct 23		Visited wagon lines. Countermarched on Br.R. Horse guard	
"	Oct 24		Spent in visiting batteries in action and digging gun pits in special positions near BEDFORD HOUSE but found nothing suitable. A demonstration over mine-craning face was given near RENINGHURST by a R.E Officer. The demonstration was attended by Lt. GEN. FANSHAWE Commanding 5th Corp, MAJ GEN. CAPPER Cmdg. 24 Div. and many other officers.	

Army Form C. 2118

100th Brigade, R.F.A.

WAR DIARY
or
INTELLIGENCE SUMMARY.
(Erase heading not required.)

Instructions regarding War Diaries and Intelligence Summaries are contained in F.S. Regs., Part II. and the Staff Manual respectively. Title pages will be prepared in manuscript.

Place	Date	Hour	Summary of Events and Information	Remarks and references to Appendices
RENINGHELST	Oct 25		Rained all day, little could be done.	
	Oct 26		Visited A & D batteries in the morning. Very clear day. Hostile aeroplanes were very busy. Two were brought down, one in our lines and one on enemy lines during a fight with our machines. Heavy firing going on the whole seems to be falling near VLAMERTINGHE. BRIG. GEN. L. H. PHILPOTTS arrived to take over command of the R.A. 24th Div.	
—	Oct 27		BRIG. GEN. SIR GODFREY THOMAS relinquished command of the R.A. 24th Div. O.C. reported 8 c.r. Hursley decided that B/109 should remain in their present wagon lines. HIS MAJESTY THE KING visited this neighbourhood accompanied by the PRINCE of WALES.	

WAR DIARY or INTELLIGENCE SUMMARY

Army Form C. 2118
109th Brigade, R.F.A.

Place	Date	Hour	Summary of Events and Information	Remarks and references to Appendices
RENINGHELST	6.6.28		The O.C., Col. J.F. CRAIG admitted to hospital. Major W.S.D. CRAVEN 7/09 assumes temporary command of the Brigade. O.C. visited gun positions and observers stations. The gun positions of B & C. which were being prepared for occupation if necessary have been temporarily abandoned. Further demolitions of mine borings Yser. Seny. west.	
"	6.8.24		O.C. visited gun positions. 2nd Lt R.M. McCULLOCH attached temporarily to 7/09 for duty. Authority obtained to draw rations for A.B.D & B.A.C. wherever obtainable. Report received from Div. H.Q. that HIS MAJESTY THE KING had met with an accident on Thursday the 28th. His horse reared and fell during an inspection of the troops. Weather conditions improved.	

109 in Bde: 1874.
Vol: 3

121/7678

24th Kurain

Nov 15

Army Form C. 2118

109th Brigade, R.F.A.
WAR DIARY
or
INTELLIGENCE SUMMARY
(Erase heading not required.)

Instructions regarding War Diaries and Intelligence Summaries are contained in F.S. Regs., Part II. and the Staff Manual respectively. Title pages will be prepared in manuscript.

Place	Date	Hour	Summary of Events and Information	Remarks and references to Appendices
RENINGHELST	Oct 30		Fine day. Batteries preparing horse shelters. Horse rugs drawn by some of the units. Quietness prevails along our front. Cordite and ballastite now being issued. O.C. 2nd forwarded a report on the unsuitability of cordite for the Howitzer Gun. and asked that ballastite only will be issued; also reported the rajves that ammunition should be grouped in order to avoid units being issued with several marks of shells. Barometer 29"14	
	Oct 31		Fall of Barometer to 28"49. Slight rain. Divine Service. Adjutant visited Officer i/c hutting accommodation and arranged to draw material when available. Huts to be built according to types approved and issued to units	

Holiday Capt RFA
Adjutant, 109th Brigade, R.F.A.

WAR DIARY or INTELLIGENCE SUMMARY

Army Form C. 2118

Place	Date	Hour	Summary of Events and Information	Remarks and references to Appendices
Reninghelst	1 November 1915		Very wet day. Barometer 28.81. O.C visited the batteries. Very quiet along the front. "Percy" the railroad gun fired several rounds at roads near DICKEBUSCH.	
"	2 Nov.		Very wet. Bar. 28.80. A/109 gun pits flooded. New positions selected close by, where pits are being made. C.R.A decided that D/109 would also be flooded out, so pits have been abandoned for a time. Two Russian prisoners escaped and got into our trenches.	
"	3rd		Showery. Bar. 28.93. G.O.C.R.A visited the wagon lines. Huts obtained a small amount of material to build huts. Preparing of horse shelters is somewhat handicapped owing to small number of G.S. Wagons available and the distance rubble has to be brought. D/109 bomb-proofs flooded out. Hostile artillery are now firing at crossroads in the neighbourhood of DICKEBUSCH with 5.9 shell chiefly.	
"	4th		Bar. 29.15. Fine. O.C attended a conference at the C.R.A. H.Q.	

W. Motacq Lieut: R.F.A.
Adjutant 109 Brigade R.F.A.

WAR DIARY
or
INTELLIGENCE SUMMARY.

Army Form C. 2118

Place	Date	Hour	Summary of Events and Information	Remarks and references to Appendices
RENINGHELST	5th Nov.		Bar. 29.24. Showery. German aeroplane brought down by one of ours in the neighbourhood of the canal. Enemy's parachutes have fallen in in several places.	
"	6th "		Bar. 29.42. Fine. O.C. accompanied by Capt. O.Dart reconnoitred new gun position near the lake at DICKEBUSCH. Hostile batteries continue to shell occasionally the cross-road VORMEZEELE-ELZENWALLE	
"	7th "		Bar. 29.41. Fine. Divine Service. Enemy occupied a good deal taking and pumping water out of their trenches. A certain amount of friendliness displayed between our men and the Germans in the opposite trenches i.e. standing up and talking.	
"	8th "		Bar. 29.21. Fine. T/F Col. S.R. Burne joined to-day and took over command of this Brigade. The O.C. visited A + B Wagon lines during the afternoon. Suggestions for improvement were noted.	

Army Form C. 2118

WAR DIARY
or
INTELLIGENCE SUMMARY.
(Erase heading not required.)

Instructions regarding War Diaries and Intelligence Summaries are contained in F. S. Regs., Part II and the Staff Manual respectively. Title pages will be prepared in manuscript.

Place	Date	Hour	Summary of Events and Information	Remarks and references to Appendices
RENINGHELST	9th Nov 1915		Bar. 28.87. Rain. High Wind. O.C. had an interview with G.O.C. 24th Division (Maj-Gen: CAPPER). O.C. visited A & D gun positions in the neighbourhood of DICKEBUSCH. O.C. had an interview with B.C.	
"	10"		Bar. 28.62. Fine morning. Hailstorm during afternoon. O.C. reconnoitred the position for a single gun at LA-CHAPELLE CHATEAU to enfilade hostile trenches near ST ELOI etc. O.C. accompanied by Adjt. inspected B/109 O.P's + wagon lines of D and B.A.C.	
"	11"		Bar. 28.96 Fine. Clear sky. O.C. and Adjt. and Capt Hart visited B/109 new gun position S.W. of DICKEBUSCH.	
"	12"		Bar. 28.30. High wind. Very wet. O.C. visited C/109th wagon lines. O.C. B.A.C. received orders from Staff Captain through this office to draw 3000 bricks from near POPERINGHE but only succeeded in obtaining 1500 to build standings for horses. During the last few days a small amount of intermittent shelling on both sides has been going on.	

2353 Wt. W2544/1454 700,000 5/15 D. D. & L. A.D.S.S./Forms/C. 2118.

WAR DIARY
or
INTELLIGENCE SUMMARY.
(Erase heading not required.)

Army Form C. 2118

Place	Date 1915	Hour	Summary of Events and Information	Remarks and references to Appendices
RENINGHELST	13th Nov	Bar 26.57 Wet.	O.C. visited A + D Batteries. Arrangements were made for O.C. D/109 to put a single gun in position near VERDRANDENMOLEN to enfilade hostile trenches etc. A small party of telephonists were sent to WATOU to undergo a short course of repair instruction etc. Reported that enemy were going to attack YPRES.	
"	14th	Bar 29.06 Fine + frosty.	O.C. and Adj: accompanied by 2/Lt Mullon reconnoitred position for B/109 as previously selected position, at present occupied by A/106th, were untenable owing to water. An observation station known as the "Brasserie" was also selected from which a good view of CHATEAU HOLLEBEKE can be obtained on the left. The mound at ST ELOI and trenches up to 9° to the right are visible. DICKEBUSCH - YPRES road from the north end of the lake to VOORMEZEELE crossroads were vigorously shelled by 8 in shells. Much damage was done to buildings and telephone wires in the vicinity of the road. A small farm just S. of the lake was also shelled. Capt. CHETWYND STAPLYTON C/107th killed by shell. 90 mules changed for horses at 13th Brigade R.F.A.	

Army Form C. 2118

WAR DIARY
or
INTELLIGENCE SUMMARY.
(Erase heading not required.)

Instructions regarding War Diaries and Intelligence Summaries are contained in F.S. Regs., Part II. and the Staff Manual respectively. Title pages will be prepared in manuscript.

Place	Date 1915	Hour	Summary of Events and Information	Remarks and references to Appendices
RENINGHELST	15th Mar		Bon. 29.15. Fine. New battle laid out from A. some distance from road. DICKEBUSCH. YPRES. Advanced Wagon Parks selected for A & D close up.	
	16th		O.C. visited D. Battery for the purpose of reconnoitring O.P's in & around 1st line trenches and stayed there during the night. Bar. 29.40. Cold. Slight showers. Frosty.	
	17th		Bar. 29.51. Fine. Occasional hail storms. Frosty. O.C. met B.R.A. at DICKEBUSCH in connection with fresh positions. Scheme for defence circulated. T 2/Lt G Phillips R.F.A. joined from England. Posted to C.	
	18th		Bar. 29.52. Fine morning. Wet afternoon. O.C. visited C. and B.A.C. Instruction received from B. Off. reference Defence Scheme for 24th D.A. All available 6 Officers attended a lecture on Aeroplane Photographs which was not very instructive. Severe Frost.	

Army Form C. 2118

WAR DIARY
or
INTELLIGENCE SUMMARY.
(Erase heading not required.)

Place	Date	Hour	Summary of Events and Information	Remarks and references to Appendices
RENINGHELST	19th Nov.		Nov. 29.19. Line & Colol. O.C accompanied by O.C. 9/109 selected positions in case of an attack by enemy. Orders received regarding move to rest area. 24th Division being relieved by 3rd Division. Staff Capt. & Adjutant inspected New Horse Shelters built at B.A.C. lines.	
"	20th "		Nov. 29.99. Lines & Firing. Orders received to move to rest area 2nd Army Col. Lamont Comdg. 30th Brigade Hors. visited our Headquarters some of the Wagon Lines. German Aeroplane came down in our lines owing to their having lost their bearings & was captured by the Canadians at HALLEBAST near KEMMEL.	
"	21st "		Nov. 30.12. Lines & Firing. Orderly Officer sent to STEENVORDE to reconnoitre roads & wagon lines. Orders received for A&D Guns in Action to be exchanged with Guns of 30th Hor. Brigade which was left at STEENVORDE ready to be taken over on arrival here. Considerable shelling by our Guns.	

Army Form C. 2118

WAR DIARY
or
INTELLIGENCE SUMMARY.
(Erase heading not required.)

Instructions regarding War Diaries and Intelligence Summaries are contained in F.S. Regs., Part II. and the Staff Manual respectively. Title pages will be prepared in manuscript.

Place	Date 1915	Hour	Summary of Events and Information	Remarks and references to Appendices
RENINGHELST	22nd	Noon	Fine Frosty with fog. Adjutant 30th Brigade visited Headquarters to make necessary arrangements for move. O.C. held a consultation with B.C's. made arrangements for move etc. Orders received to dump 108 rounds per Gun A&D Batteries.	
"	23rd		Mar 29.60. Wet. A Battery were shelled. O.C. visited wagon lines. Horses in good condition.	
"	24th		Mar 29.65. Fine and warmer. B&C Batteries move off to STEENVORDE at about 3.30 p.m. Battery of the Brigade moved into A wagon line before they were due to leave.	
"	25th		Mar ? Showers. Headquarters A&D Batteries with B.A.C. moved to STEENVORDE. A difficult march owing to congestion of traffic. D who was last Battery did not arrive until 3.30 A.M. 26th.	

WAR DIARY
or
INTELLIGENCE SUMMARY.
(Erase heading not required.)

Army Form C. 2118

Place	Date	Hour	Summary of Events and Information	Remarks and references to Appendices
STEENVORDE	26th Nov		Fine. Sharp frost wind. The Brigade remained in billets. A billeting party was sent on to OCHTEZEELE to arrange billets for the 28th then proceeded on to NORTBECOURT to arrange final billets.	
"	27th		Brigade moved off at 10.0 AM to OCHTEZEELE marching via ST. SYLVESTRE - QUAESTRAETE - S. of CASSEL and reached billets at 2.30 p.m. Billets above the average. Genl. Headlam, accompanied by C.R.A. inspected Brigade near CASSEL. Sharp frost.	
NORTBECOURT	28th		Sharp frost. Brigade marched off at 9 am. passing through CROME STRAETE. WATTEN. EPERLECQUES. to NORTBECOURT and reached billets by 4.30 p.m. Great delay occurred between Cross roads 1 mile E of CROME STRAETE owing to continual blocking of the roads by baggage wagons hundred wagons and carts of the 106. 107. 108 Brigades. The vehicles of these brigades had got mixed up and owing to the slippery	

WAR DIARY
or
INTELLIGENCE SUMMARY.
(*Erase heading not required.*)

Army Form C. 2118

Place	Date	Hour	Summary of Events and Information	Remarks and references to Appendices
NORTBECOURT	28th	Nov	continued:— State of the roads, from condition of some of the horses, and bad driving were often stuck fast in the ditches. G.O.C. 24th Division accompanied by C.R.A. inspected the Brigade at a point about 2 miles E of WATTEN and saw the whole state of affairs. The Brigade marched obediently, keeping well together. The baggage Wagons which always marched in rear of the Brigade marched in good order under Lt. D. Stalker. B.A.C. were all in their billets by 5 p.m. Unsatisfactory arrangements were made for collection & delivery of mails.	
"	29th	"	Frosty. Country very hilly. Indifferent billets except B.A.C. had water supply. O.C. billeted B.A.C.	
"	30th	"	Bar 28.36. Change much milder, slight rain. O.C. visited B & D batteries programme of training arranged whilst in rest area.	

N. Hockey Lieut. R.F.A.
Adjutant 109 Brigade R.F.A.

Aj 7/7

R.T.O
    ABEELE

About 18 reinforcements arrive for us at POPERINGHE at 14.26 to day.

As ABEELE is very much nearer it would be a great convenience if we could meet them there.

Is this possible please?

Nelson Zambra
Lieut. R.F.A.
Adjutant 24th Divisional Ammunition Column.

1 - 11 - 15

You can delivery them here if it is possible that you to arrange to meet them, we have no advise of Train

Sapper Bowers
Le 9 R 70

"A" Form.   Army Form C. 2121.

MESSAGES AND SIGNALS.   No. of Message

App 13

Prefix...... Code...... m. | Words | Charge | This message is on a/c of: | Recd. at...... m.
Office of Origin and Service Instructions. | | | | Date
 | Sent | | ...... Service | From
 | At...... m. | | |
 | To | | (Signature of "Franking Officer.") | By
 | By | | |

TO { 24ᵀᴴ D.A.C.

Sender's Number.	Day of Month.	In reply to Number	AAA
BM 158	9ᵗʰ		

Reference B 27 and 28 1/40.000 map
24ᵗʰ D.A.C. will move tomorrow
into new billets
  Starting point INN 1 mile N of
WATOU 10 AM
  Route via WATOU — ABEELE
HQ & No 1 section to R 9 B 28
  No 2 section to R 10 C 04
  No 3 section to R 1 D 56
Order of march No 2 No 1 No 3
17ᵗʰ D.A.C. vacate their billets today
24ᵗʰ DAC will occupy ground which
corresponding sections of 17ᵗʰ DAC now
occupy aaa 24ᵗʰ DAC will bring with
them any tents left behind by 106ᵗʰ & 107ᵗʰ
brigades aaa Lorries will collect these
at cross roads guard will come in with lorries

From BM 24 Div Art
Place
Time 4.55 pm   J P Harvey
                               Major

The above may be forwarded as now corrected. (Z)

Censor.   Signature of Addressee or person authorised to telegraph in his name.
* This line should be erased if not required.

APP 13

The guard on the tents of the 108
& 109 Btns will remain on duty until
~~the tents are removed in~~ lorries
come to fetch the tents — The
guard will then be brought along in the
lorries —

"C" Form (Original).			Army Form C. 2123.
MESSAGES AND SIGNALS.		No. of Message	

Prefix	Code	Words 37	Received From LCO By Jamieson	Sent, or sent out At ... m. To ... By	Office Stamp.
Charges to collect					
Service Instructions.					

Handed in at LCO Office 1.33 p.m. Received 2.18 p.m.

TO 24th DAC

Sender's Number G12	Day of Month 30	In reply to Number	AAA

24th DAC will move tomorrow morning at 5.30 am to rejoin the Division marching by BEUVRY—BETHUNE—CHOQUES—LILLERS aaa addsd 24th DAC Repts BGRA 24th Div acknowledge

FROM PLACE & TIME: 11 Corps 1.30 pm

log Is Rdr: DPd.
vol: 4

12/909

WAR DIARY
or
INTELLIGENCE SUMMARY.
(Erase heading not required.)

Army Form C. 2118.

Place	Date	Hour	Summary of Events and Information	Remarks and references to Appendices
1915. NORTBECOURT.	Dec. 1st		Bar. 29.32. Showery. O.C. visited 6 & 9 Batteries. Horses generally in good condition. Orders received to move to AUDREHEM - CLERQUES Area by St LOUIS river. HEM	
	2nd		Bar. 29.70. Lieut. Clapp (old returned) was ordered to remain in present billets, pending orders to the 131st Brigade area in the Canadian division at KEMMEL. The Brigade spent the day in packing up ready for move to new billets. Major Connan went on leave.	
	3rd		Bar. 29.67. Mostly overcast. Brigade moved to new Billeting area at AUDREHEM - CLERQUES. Billets fairly comfortable. Headquarters, A & B.A.C. horses under cover. B & D half under cover. Water excellent.	
	4th		Bar. 28.45. very wet. Brigade spent the day settling in billets & fetching heavy baggage from a dump left at their old billets.	

Army Form C. 2118.

WAR DIARY
or
INTELLIGENCE SUMMARY.
(Erase heading not required.)

Place	Date	Hour	Summary of Events and Information	Remarks and references to Appendices
AUDENFORT	Dec 5th		Bar 28.72. Showery. One Sub Section of the B.A.C. went to WATTEN, having been ordered to join 131st How. Bde. It consisted of 21. N.C.O.s men 24 horses 2 mules and 4 Ammn Wagons, one filled with 48 rounds of B. and 3 filled with 144 of B.x, the remaining 1 Tennant of Brigade H.Q. waited on.	
"	6th		Bar 28.51. High Wind. Wet. Brigade Headquarters (Wagon lines) move from AUDREHEM to AUDENFORT to make room for 1 section of A Battery. B. Bty played D at football, winning by 3-1. This match took place in connection with the Divisional Tournament. A test B.A.C. S-1 Horses amiths, 1 Gunner + 1 Driver posted to the Brigade from D.A.C.	
"	7th		Bar 28.47. Wet. D Battery moved into HAMEL near Clerques, by this arrangement nearly all the horses in the Brigade are now under cover. Men's billets are fairly comfortable	

WAR DIARY

or

INTELLIGENCE SUMMARY.

Place	Date	Hour	Summary of Events and Information	Remarks and references to Appendices
	1915			
AUDENFORT	8th December		Bar 28.85" Fine. A & B Batteries played the final football tie of the Brigade. A Bty winning by 5-0 qualified to represent 109th Brigade in the Divisional Competition. Lecture by O.C. to Officers & selected N.C.O.s. Subjects "March Discipline & Observing".	
"	9th Decr		Bar 29.00. Very Wet. Brig.-Genl PHILPOTTS inspected men's billets and also stables.	
"	10th "		Bar 26.74 Variable. Lecture by O.C. to Officers & N.C.O's on "The observation of fire". In the afternoon a lecture by Major Genl CAPPER to all Officers & N.C.O's, also a general of new. The subject was "Discipline & the care of equipment". H.Holiday 2nd Rolyland, went on leave.	
"	11th "		Bar 28.82 Showery. 13 Remounts (I.D.) arrived. All, with the exception of 3 were eminently suitable for Artillery work.	

Army Form C. 2118.

WAR DIARY
or
INTELLIGENCE SUMMARY.
(Erase heading not required.)

Place	Date	Hour	Summary of Events and Information	Remarks and references to Appendices
	1915			
AUDENFORT	12 Dec		Bar 29.20 Fine. A Bty. played the D.A.C at QUELMES winning by 3-1	
"	13 "		Bar 29.25 Fine. Nothing of importance	
"	14 "		Bar 29.41 Fine. Frosty morning. Selected Officers & Q.M.S. of the Brigade attended a lecture at ALQUINES by S.S.O. 2nd Division. The subject being "Supplies"	
"	15 "		Bar 29.50 Wet. Very thorough inspection by G.O.C, R.A., of men's billets, recreation rooms, gun parks, stabling, and harness. The result was most satisfactory	
"	16 "		Bar 29.20 Dull. Brigade skeleton scheme, practicing Brigade and Battery Staffs & their communications	

Army Form C. 2118.

WAR DIARY
or
INTELLIGENCE SUMMARY.

(Erase heading not required.)

Instructions regarding War Diaries and Intelligence Summaries are contained in F. S. Regs., Part II. and the Staff Manual respectively. Title pages will be prepared in manuscript.

Place	Date	Hour	Summary of Events and Information	Remarks and references to Appendices
AUDENFORT	17th Dec.		Bar. 58.95. Fine. Inspection by Lt. Gen. Sir H. PLUMER Comdg 2nd Army of all units of the Brigade in their billets. Capt. Hart went on leave. R.S.M. Watkins ordered to leave on receiving his commission.	
"	18 "		Bar. 29.24 Fine. Nothing of importance.	
"	19 "		Bar. 29.49 Fine. Nothing of importance.	
"	20 "		Bar. 29.50 Wet. Usual routine drills etc. 8 Gunners & Drivers & 1 S/Smith joined from D.A.C.	
"	21 "		Bar. 29.05 Wet. Lecture by O.C. R.A. Final tie between A/109 and C/109 for Divisional Football Competition. Result A/109 3 C/109 2. B.S.M. Walker joined on promotion.	
"	22 "		Bar. 29.09 Wet. Brigade Route March. Capt. Shaw went on leave.	

2353 Wt. W2344/1454 700,000 5/15 D.D. & L. A.D.S.S./Forms/C. 2118.

WAR DIARY
or
INTELLIGENCE SUMMARY.

Army Form C. 2118

Place	Date	Hour	Summary of Events and Information	Remarks and references to Appendices
AUDENFORT	23rd Dec.		Bar. 29.11 Showery. Usual routine. O.C. went to NORDASQUES attend a lecture given by a Colonel from 49th Division. A/109 beaten by Glasgow Yeomanry 4-0 in the semi-final of Divisional Competition	
"	24		Bar. 29.15. Showery. Instructions received regarding relief of 49th Division by the 2nd Division.	
"	25		Bar. 29.24. Fine. Headquarters played B.A.C. football in the morning + lost 6-0. Batteries held sports. Orders received to march from rest area on the 27th. Divisional Supply Wagons ordered to return on the 26th.	
"	26		Bar. 29.30. Fine. Divine Service	
"	27		Bar. 29.45. High Wind. Usual routine	

Army Form C. 2118.

WAR DIARY
or
INTELLIGENCE SUMMARY.
(Erase heading not required.)

Instructions regarding War Diaries and Intelligence Summaries are contained in F. S. Regs., Part II. and the Staff Manual respectively. Title pages will be prepared in manuscript.

Place	Date	Hour	Summary of Events and Information	Remarks and references to Appendices
AUDENFORT	28th Dec.	Bar 29.52	High Wind. Brigade & Battery Staff scheme.	
"	29th "	Bar 29.49	Fine. Orders received to relieve 17th Division	
"	30 " "	Bar 29.50	Fine Nothing of importance	
"	31st "	Bar 29.15	Fine Packing up. Orders received to march on 1 Jan 1916	

H Holday 2nd R.T.A.
Adjutant 109th bde R.F.A.

109 D/Bde: RFA.
Vol: 5

Two—

24

109th Brigade R.F.A.

Army Form C. 2118.

WAR DIARY
or
INTELLIGENCE SUMMARY.
(Erase heading not required.)

Instructions regarding War Diaries and Intelligence Summaries are contained in F. S. Regs., Part II. and the Staff Manual respectively. Title pages will be prepared in manuscript.

Place	Date 1916	Hour	Summary of Events and Information	Remarks and references to Appendices
AUDENFORT	Jany.	1st	Bar. 29.16. Wet. High wind. Brigade Marched to BUYSSCHUERE via Sergues and LE-BAS. difficulties arose owing to the Bullets not being properly remounted.	
BUYSSCHUERE	—	2nd	Bar. 29.37. Wet. Brigade marched to STEENVOORDE via CASSEL. B.M. met O.C. conducted him by Motor car to B.H.Q. at the firing line Brigade marched up the Steep Cassel Hill admirably. Lieut Stalker proceeded on Leave. H.N	
STEENVOORDE	—	3rd	Bar. 29.50 fine. 1st Section of A + B. moved up to the Wagon Lines of B + C. 81st Brigade R.F.A. Personnel Proceeded by Bus (Motor) to firing line in relief that night. Personnel of 81st returning to ARNEKE by the same Bus. Adjutant + Telephonists proceeded to B.H.Q. to join O.C. at H24D99. Chalion Ferri. O.C. reconnoitred the country.	
—	—	4th	Bar 29.48. Dry 60°F. Remainder of B.H.Q. 2nd Section of A + B.D Battery in reserve + B.A.C. marched to Wagon Lines 1½ miles S.E. of POPERINGHE. Personnel of 2nd Section A + B were taken by Bus to Gun Positions at A/109. I.D.362. B/109 I.21a.31. Orderly officer + M.O. arrived at BHQ firing line same day. O.C. + Adjt. took over from BHQ 81st Bde. who left for home by Bus at 7 p.m. Country reconnoitred by O.C. + B/Cs. Lieut A. Clarke proceeded on leave. H.N	

109th Brigade R.F.A.

WAR DIARY
or
INTELLIGENCE SUMMARY.

Army Form C. 2118.

Place	Date	Hour	Summary of Events and Information	Remarks and references to Appendices
Ensingham	Jany 5th		Bar. 29.51. Fine. Communications more thoroughly reconnoitred. Retaliation A. by B/109.	
	6th		Bar. 29.54. Dull. 14th D.A. taken over by 24th D.A. at 10.A.M. Communications indifferent.	
	7th		Bar. 29.68. Dull. A/109 informing Gun positions. H.Q. informing Telephone Dugout, which had fallen in. B.H.Q. Shelled by 5.9. No Casualties. Retaliation A(C1) by B/109.	
	8th		Bar. 29.64. Bright. O.C. visited Batteries in Action.	
	9th		Bar. 29.71. Bright. Adjutant reconnoitred Canal Bank for laying Telephone Wires very suitable good protection. Retaliation on Trench Mortar opposite C+4 118 by 6th Siege + B/109. Effective fire reported by F Surveys. C.R.A + B Major visited B.H.Q. Heavy barrage opposite front trenches 9.am. 11th N	
	10th		Bar. 29.74. Dull. Intermittent shelling on both sides. Communications unimproved	

109th Brigade RFA.

Army Form C. 2118.

WAR DIARY
or
INTELLIGENCE SUMMARY.

(Erase heading not required.)

Instructions regarding War Diaries and Intelligence Summaries are contained in F. S. Regs., Part II. and the Staff Manual respectively. Title pages will be prepared in manuscript.

Place	Date	Hour	Summary of Events and Information	Remarks and references to Appendices
Firing Line Jany	11th	Dull.	Mar 29.48. Dull. Retaliation called for four times during the day by 72nd Infty Bde. Communications improved. G.O.C. 24th Div visited A/109.	
	12th		Mar 29.65. Bright. Aeroplanes very busy. Two Hostile planes over, our panels while very difficult to see except when turning when the Sun rays caught it. Retaliation called for by 72nd Infty Bde.	
	13th		Mar 29.10. Cold wind. Showery. Nothing unusual.	
	14th		Mar 29.55. Fine. Nothing of Interest. Lt. Kerr proceeded on leave. U.K	
	15th		Mar 29.41. Fine. O.C. reconnoitred new observing Stations in connection with a Group Scheme.	
	16th		Mar 29.53 Fine Nothing Unusual. Hostile Guns very quiet.	

109th Brigade R.F.A.

Army Form C. 2118.

WAR DIARY
or
INTELLIGENCE SUMMARY.

Place	Date	Hour	Summary of Events and Information	Remarks and references to Appendices
Trompe[...]	Jany 17th	11th	Mar. 29.31. Fine. Re-arrangement of Group system. A/109 now become part of Left Group, under Lt Col R. L. Bates. B/109 under Right Group under Lt Col Wastall R.F.A. B.H.Q. less a small party in charge proceeded to POPERINGHE	
-"-		18th		
Poperinghe		18th	Bar. 29.35. Fine. O.C. 9 Rifle shelled wagon lines. B/109 very bad, mud practically knee deep and no roads of approach.	
-"-		19th	Bar 29.39. Dull. Enemy shelled Wagon Lines with a Naval Gun from the direction of PILKIEM. about 45 rounds 6 inch shells. No damage done.	
-"-		20	Bar. 29.44. Fine. Lt Col S.P. Divine proceeded on leave. Major J. De L Cowan assumed command temporarily.	
-"-		21st	Bar. 29.52. Dull. R.S.M. Walker promoted to 2/Lt. on the 9th of Jany 1916. B.S.M. Ruston promoted R.S.M. on the 21st of Jany 1916.	

109th Brigade R.F.A.

Army Form C. 2118.

WAR DIARY
or
INTELLIGENCE SUMMARY.
(Erase heading not required.)

Instructions regarding War Diaries and Intelligence Summaries are contained in F. S. Regs., Part II and the Staff Manual respectively. Title pages will be prepared in manuscript.

Place	Date	Hour	Summary of Events and Information	Remarks and references to Appendices
POPERINGHE	Jany 22nd		Nothing of Importance.	
"	23.		At 12.15 AM. Hostile Aeroplane flew over & dropped 4 Bombs in POPERINGHE. No damage done. 2 Killed.	
"	24th		Nothing of Importance.	
"	25th		O.C. visited all wagon lines. 2 Chargers & 10 L.D. Horses came.	
"	26.		O.C. & Adjt. visited Right Group Headquarters at ZILLEBEKE LAKE & A&B Batteries 109th Brigade R.F.A. all very quiet.	
"	27.		Nothing Unusual.	
"	28.		G.O.C. 24th Div. accompanied by G.O.C. R.A. visited wagon lines. (O.C.) Lt Col E.R. Burne D.S.O. returned & visited wagon lines	

109th Brigade R.F.A.

Army Form C. 2118.

WAR DIARY
or
INTELLIGENCE SUMMARY.
(Erase heading not required.)

Place	Date	Hour	Summary of Events and Information	Remarks and references to Appendices
POPERINGHE	Jany 29.		Nothing unusual.	
"	30.		B.H.Q. moved up to Chateau H24D77. O.C. & Adjt. went on to ZILLEBEKE LAKE to commence taking over the right Group. R.A. from O.C. 108th Brigade R.F.A.	
Firing Line	31.		Taking over of right Group completed by 2-30 P.M. B.H.Q. 108th B'de moved to Wagon Lines near POPERINGHE. B.H.Q. 109 moved into Dug outs at ZILLEBEKE LAKE.	

K Mahony Lt R.F.A.
Adjutant, 109th Brigade, R.F.A.

Log L Bde RFA
Vol: 6

24

109th Brigade R.F.A

Army Form C. 2118.

WAR DIARY
or
INTELLIGENCE SUMMARY.
(Erase heading not required.)

Place	Date	Hour	Summary of Events and Information	Remarks and references to Appendices
Firing Line 1916	1st Feby.		Fine. Arrangements made by R.G. in combination with H.A.R. to demolish some strong points, communication trenches, dumps etc.	
"	2		Fine. Nothing of Importance	
"	3		Bright. Five of our aeroplanes returned about 9.30. apparently from a raid. They were vigorously shelled but they returned safely. Hostile aeroplanes were busy later which in some way prevented the Guns of R. Group carrying out their allotted task.	
"	4		Wet & High wind. Hostile Guns very active shelling Gun positions, Dumps & Dug-outs which no doubt was in retaliation to our shelling behind their lines on the 1st. 30 rounds of 6.9 How. were fired at Dug-outs on the ZILLEBEKE LAKE occupied by 109th Brigade Headquarters R.A. Right Group, but luckily no casualties were caused.	

109th Brigade R.F.A.

Army Form C. 2118.

WAR DIARY
or
INTELLIGENCE SUMMARY.
(Erase heading not required.)

Instructions regarding War Diaries and Intelligence Summaries are contained in F. S. Regs., Part II. and the Staff Manual respectively. Title pages will be prepared in manuscript.

Place	Date 1916	Hour	Summary of Events and Information	Remarks and references to Appendices
Firing Line	5th Feby	Fine.	Hostile aeroplane was deceived by puffs fired from an old Gun positions as about two hours later about 200 shells of all calibres were fired at the positions.	
"	6th	"	Dull. Infantry dug outs near Belgian Chateau & YPRES shelled by 5.9 guns vigorously which caused a few casualties. This 15cm or 5.9 battery has now been located & engaged with our 4.5 How. Otherwise fairly quiet.	
"	7th	"	Fine. Intermittent shelling on both sides. Hostile aeroplanes very active.	
"	8th	"	Fine. ZILLEBEKE LAKE dug outs shelled causing a few casualties. Hostile Batteries firing at night located by flash spotter & silenced by our 4.5 Hows. G.O.C. 24th Division visited Group Headquarters. Hostile Aeroplanes very active. One thought down near POPERINGHE by Anti-Aircraft Guns. HOOGE trenches heavily shelled by enemy which no doubt was done to draw our fire to enable their aeroplanes to spot our Batteries	

109th Brigade R.F.A.

Army Form C. 2118.

WAR DIARY
or
INTELLIGENCE SUMMARY.

(Erase heading not required.)

Place	Date	Hour	Summary of Events and Information	Remarks and references to Appendices
Liningtoue	9th Sept.		Fine. Hostile 15 C.M. battery fired on B/109 at daybreak, no damage. Some were GAS. Shells which affected our eyes at the ZILLEBEKE LAKE some 500 yards away from where the shells were bursting. Hostile Aeroplanes very active.	
"	10th	"	Fine. Hostile Artillery very active. During the night Right Group called upon the H.A.R. to silence enemies Batteries who were shelling YPRES & ZILLEBEKE LAKE vigorously.	
"	11th	"	Wet. G.O.C. R.A. 24th Divst Arty visited Right Group H.Q & some of the Batteries. He was accompanied by the new Brigade Major. (Capt A.W. Griffsen R.F.A.)	
"	12th	"	Wet & Dull. Hostile Artillery active in the YPRES. area.	

109th Brigade R.F.A.

Army Form C. 2118.

WAR DIARY
or
INTELLIGENCE SUMMARY.

(Erase heading not required.)

Place	Date	Hour	Summary of Events and Information	Remarks and references to Appendices
Ypres Area	Feby	13th	Fine. Violent bombardment of our Trenches just N of the HOOGE - MENIN. road from 4 am until 3.30 p.m. Our Infantry holding that portion were forced to retire to their second line until the evening. The greater part of the shelling was directed from the flanks. Enemy appears to have cleared his front line for that purpose. Trenches were badly damaged though the shooting generally was not very accurate. It is estimated 8,000 shells of various calibre were fired. Our Artillery held the show well in hand in case of an Infantry attack.	
		14th	Fine. A bombardment of the enemies trenches opposite those tranches of ours shelled the previous day was carried out this morning and were very successful. Enemy bombarded our Trenches at HOOGE from 3.30 p.m until 5.30 p.m very heavily. The S.O.S. rocket signal was sent up at 5.15 p.m. and in 35 seconds after the signal our artillery formed a barrage and although the enemy was seen to climb up on to his parapet he was prevented from leaving his trenches. A barrage was then formed by the enemies guns behind our lines. The attack failed and firing practically ceased by 7 p.m. 2/Lt J.S. Peare slightly wounded. A few other casualties.	

109th Brigade R.F.A.

Army Form C. 2118.

WAR DIARY
or
INTELLIGENCE SUMMARY.
(Erase heading not required.)

Instructions regarding War Diaries and Intelligence Summaries are contained in F. S. Regs., Part II. and the Staff Manual respectively. Title pages will be prepared in manuscript.

Place	Date	Hour	Summary of Events and Information	Remarks and references to Appendices
Zonnebeke	Feby 15		Very little shelling except a few bursts of fire at HOOGE trenches but ceased on our retaliating. At 8 p.m. a continued Artillery Bombardment commenced on trenches captured by the enemy. One trench was retaken during the night.	
"	16		Wet. 109th B.H.Q. relieved by 108th B.H.Q. and returned to billets at POPERINGHE. All quiet on both sides.	
POPERINGHE	17		High Wind. O.C. visited Wagon Lines. Hostile aeroplane dropped bombs on POPERINGHE area. Very little damage.	
"	18		High Wind. O.C. visited Wagon Lines. & G.O.C. R.A.	
"	19		Fine. Nothing unusual. Extract taken from 24th Divn Special order No 39. G.O.C. division desires to add his congratulations from Army Comdr & Corps Comdr; his appreciation of the conduct of the Right Group R.F.A. whose instant action and accurate fire materially assisted the Infantry in rendering the enemy's attack on HOOGE abortive	

109th Brigade R.F.A.

Army Form C. 2118.

WAR DIARY
or
INTELLIGENCE SUMMARY.

Place	Date	Hour	Summary of Events and Information	Remarks and references to Appendices
POPERINGHE	Feby 20th	Fine	POPERINGHE was bombed from Aeroplanes at 6.30 A.M. no damage. O.C visited D/109 Wagon Lines.	
"	21st	Fine.	POPERINGHE bombed after mid-night. Lt. Douglas took over as Actg/Adjutant. Lieut. Holoday proceeded to B/109 Gun Position. Lt. Saunders reported and attached B/109.Bde.	
"	22.	Cold.	POPERINGHE Station shelled at 4.50 a.m. and during day. O.C visited B&A. Wagon Lines. Right Group Headquarters shelled and direct hit obtained on dug outs, causing some casualties.	
"	23.	Cold.	POPERINGHE bombed soon after mid-night, raiders fired upon by Anti-Aircraft guns. O.C. visited B.A.C. Headquarters and A Battery.	

109th Brigade, R.F.A.

Army Form C. 2118.

WAR DIARY
or
INTELLIGENCE SUMMARY.
(Erase heading not required.)

Instructions regarding War Diaries and Intelligence Summaries are contained in F. S. Regs., Part II. and the Staff Manual respectively. Title pages will be prepared in manuscript.

Place	Date	Hour	Summary of Events and Information	Remarks and references to Appendices
POPERINGHE	Feby 24th	Cold.	O visited B/109th Wagon Lines. Capt. Short returned from gun position to rest. All leave cancelled. D/109 came out of action.	
"	25th	Cold.	F.G.C.M. Bdr. Bell, A/109th. O.C. visited A/109th Bde.	
"	26th	Cold.	POPERINGHE bombed early in the morning about 6 a.m. O.C. visited A/109 wagon lines.	
"	27th	Windy.	Nothing to report.	
"	28th	Cold.	O.C. reconnoitred new defence positions for Bde with Major Cowan.	
"	29th	Bright.	Nothing to report.	

A.M. Douglas Lieut. R.F.A.
Adjt. 109th Brigade. R.F.A.

109 RFA
Vol 7

24

109th Brigade R.F.A.

Army Form C. 2118.

WAR DIARY
or
INTELLIGENCE SUMMARY.
(Erase heading not required.)

Place	Date 1916	Hour	Summary of Events and Information	Remarks and references to Appendices
POPERINGHE	March 1st		Lieut. Leach A.V.C. left on 10 days Special Leave. Lt. McGregor A.V.C. took charge. C.O. visited C.R.A.	
"	2		Capt. Hart and Lt. Saunders went up to B/109 Guns. C.O. visited A & B. Battery wagon Lines, and lectured to Infantry Officers in the evening.	
"	3		C.O. visited Wagon Lines.	
Reningher	4		Lt. Col. Burne took over Right Group.	
"	5		C.O. visited Batteries of R. Group. Enemy Artillery quiet. Nothing to report.	
"	6		C.O. visited Trenches with 6st Skinner in afternoon. Adjt. visited A/108 & B/109. Quiet generally on Front. Generals lecture at POPERINGHE.	
"	7		C.O. visited Batteries. Nothing to Report.	

109th Brigade R.F.A.

Army Form C. 2118.

WAR DIARY
or
INTELLIGENCE SUMMARY.
(Erase heading not required.)

Instructions regarding War Diaries and Intelligence Summaries are contained in F. S. Regs., Part II and the Staff Manual respectively. Title pages will be prepared in manuscript.

Place	Date	Hour	Summary of Events and Information	Remarks and references to Appendices
Ferring June	8.		L.O. visited Batteries with O.O.	
"	9		G.O.C. R.A. visited Headquarters. Quiet generally.	
"	10.		Observation plane brought down by Fokker machine while working for B/109 Bde.	
"	11.		Lt Col Burne handed over Left Group to Lt Col Wallhall and took over Right Group with 109th Bde Staff from 50th Divn at Belgian Chateau.	
"	12.		Adjt 109th Bde went to 19th Infty Bde Headquarters as Liason Officer. Quiet generally.	
"	13.		Much aeroplane activity.	
"	14		Enemy shelled B trenches heavily at 1 p.m. Group retaliation effective.	

109th Brigade R.F.A.

Army Form C. 2118.

WAR DIARY
or
INTELLIGENCE SUMMARY.
(Erase heading not required.)

Instructions regarding War Diaries and Intelligence Summaries are contained in F. S. Regs., Part II. and the Staff Manual respectively. Title pages will be prepared in manuscript.

Place	Date	Hour	Summary of Events and Information	Remarks and references to Appendices
In the Field	15.		HOOGE Shelled at 11 am and again at 1 pm. Both Groups retaliated.	
"	16.		Aeroplane activity. B trenches and supports shelled at 1 pm. Group retaliation.	
"	17th		Fired with 6th Siege on trenches and works behind BIRD CAGE. Enemy very active during day with Gas Shells round YPRES. 1 Section of Batteries relieved by Lahore Divn.	
"	18.		Relief completed. Col Dunne handed over to Col Macswell. Headquarters Shelled also Batteries Right Group. Arrived rest Billets at STEENVORDE about 11 pm.	
STEENVORDE	19.		C.O visited wagon lines and D.A. Headquarters.	
"	20.		C.O visited wagon lines.	

109th Brigade. R.F.A.

Army Form C. 2118.

WAR DIARY
or
INTELLIGENCE SUMMARY.
(Erase heading not required.)

Place	Date	Hour	Summary of Events and Information	Remarks and references to Appendices
STEENVOORDE	March 21		C.O. visited wagon lines.	
"	" 22		Remained in Rest Area. B.C's visited area around Hell 63, on 27th & 28th	
"	" 10 to 31st		with view of taking over from 1st Canadian Division.	

W. Parkin.
Lieut: R.F.A.
for Adjutant 109 Brigade R.F.A.

109th Brigade R.F.A.

XXV

109 RFA
Vol 8

Army Form C. 2118.

WAR DIARY
or
INTELLIGENCE SUMMARY.
(Erase heading not required.)

Place	Date	Hour	Summary of Events and Information	Remarks and references to Appendices
Firing Line 1916	April 1st		The Left Section of Batteries & B.A.C. left for Hill 63. at 10 A.M. Head Quarters Staff being at the Head of the Bethune-Wulverghem road passed CASTRE Rly. STN. at 10.30 a.m.	
	2nd		O.B. inspected all gun positions. C.R.C.R.A. visited Brigade H.Q.	
	3rd		O.C. attended conference of B'des with D.A. Staff at H.Q's of 109 Bde. and afterwards inspected all wagon lines and issued instructions re improvements.	
	4		2nd Lt. Botham D/109. left to join Trench Mortar Battery. Reports on nightly lines of Howitzers sent to D.A.	
	5th		O.C. visited all Batteries. Premature occurred 30 yards from the muzzle of a Gun of D/109. no damage done. A faulty fuze No 100: 2 fuze was the cause of the premature.	

109th Brigade R.F.A

Army Form C. 2118.

WAR DIARY
or
INTELLIGENCE SUMMARY.
(Erase heading not required.)

Instructions regarding War Diaries and Intelligence Summaries are contained in F. S. Regs., Part II. and the Staff Manual respectively. Title pages will be prepared in manuscript.

Place	Date	Hour	Summary of Events and Information	Remarks and references to Appendices
Grenpue	April 6th		O.C. visited all Batteries and afterwards accompanied Col Coates act/G.O.C.R.A. (was Genl. Phillpotts on leave) round 109th Bde. Waggon Lines. Notification was received from D.A. that G.O.C. D.A. Corps will inspect A & B/109 gun positions tomorrow 7th. A/109 report 2 prematures H.E. shell 100 fuzes 2 guns, 2 men of the Northamptons who were some distance away were wounded, occurrence reported to D.A. Inquiry will be held into same.	
	7th		D.A. notify that Huge Inspect. (Major Elliott) will attend B.A.C. at 11 a.m. to fuze shell for experimental purposes with 106 & 101 fuze, shooting not to be arranged for tomorrow.	
	8th		G.O.C. R.A. Corps visited gun positions of Batteries of 109th Bde. Major Elliott visited B.A.C. and fuzed 30 shells 106 & 101 fuze Amm. Col to take shells to D/109. In the afternoon a trial of the fuzes took place. The shells were fired into hard & soft ground and directly compared with the present No 100 fuze - which were fired alongside. 2 Bursts occurred with fuze 100 but none with either of the new fuzes. The 101 fuze is really only the 100 fuze with delay action taken out and the cock pallet removed. Court of Inquiry held re cause of 2 prematures in guns at A/109.	

109th Brigade R.F.A.

Army Form C. 2118.

WAR DIARY
or
INTELLIGENCE SUMMARY.
(Erase heading not required.)

Instructions regarding War Diaries and Intelligence Summaries are contained in F. S. Regs., Part II. and the Staff Manual respectively. Title pages will be prepared in manuscript.

Place	Date	Hour	Summary of Events and Information	Remarks and references to Appendices
Strazeele	April 8th		O.C. visited Gun Positions. Regimental Board sat on inquiry as to unfit clothing. The following 2nd Lts were Gazetted 1st Lts on this date. R. McC. Bulloch. J. de Barclay. H. Milton. N.C. Lockhart.	
—	9th		O.C. visited Gun positions. Genl Capper visited O.P.s A. & B. Batteries. 1 new draft of 6 Gunners & 6 Drivers received from D.A.C.	
—	10th		O.C. accompanied by Capt Gardner A/109 visited alternate Gun Positions forward & afterwards visited Wagon Lines.	
—	11th		O.C. visited all Batteries. Reconnaissance of new positions for wagon lines of the Brigade by Capt Shaw & 2/Lt Davis of B.A.C./109.	
—	12th		Labelling of telephone wires proceeded with. Further reconnaissance by Capt Shaw of new wagon Lines. Report by O.C. to the Staff Captain re new wagon lines.	

109 Brigade R.F.A.

Army Form C. 2118.

WAR DIARY
or
INTELLIGENCE SUMMARY.
(Erase heading not required.)

Place	Date	Hour	Summary of Events and Information	Remarks and references to Appendices
Wagon Line	April 13th	13h	Court of Inquiry held to investigate death of No 17289 Dr J. Seymour B/109.	
-	-	14h	O.C. visited & inspected Wagon Lines & O.P.s	
-	-	15h	O.C. visited Batteries Wagon Lines. H.Q. D.A. move to BAILLEUL.	
-	-	16h	Lorries for all Officers received for HILL 63, & issued to Batteries. Store Dump decided upon at B.3.D.2.8. (D/109 Wagon Lines) O.C. visited Batteries. Report furnished by O.C. to Brigade Major on extreme concealment 3 guns of D/109.	
-	-	17h	Statement of Sore Joints furnished by O.C. to Brigade Major. O.C. visited Batteries & O.Ps & reports necessity of cutting down trees on the WULVERGHEM-MESSINES, road for better observation.	
-	-	18	Trial of No 106 fuzes mixed with 100. % of latter, being duds on soft ground the 106 very satisfactory. Draft of 2 Gunners & 3 Drivers received from D.A.C.	

109th (How.) Brigade R.F.A.

Army Form C. 2118.

WAR DIARY
or
INTELLIGENCE SUMMARY.

Place	Date	Hour	Summary of Events and Information	Remarks and references to Appendices
Firing Line	April 19	14	L.D. Horses received & appointed between Batteries & O.Ps. O.C. visited Batteries & O.Ps. Inspection of Wagon Lines. Enemy Artillery N.E. of MESSINES persistent. Trench Mortar in left Sector quiet till 4.15 pm when it opened fire & was engaged.	
		20	O.C. visits all Batteries & O.Ps & Inspected work at Wagon Lines.	
		21	Applications from Majors & Captains in the Brigade invited for work in Munitions Dept. London. Capt London, Capt Shaw B.A.C. only applicants who wished his name submitted. Submitted accordingly.	
		22	Trench Mortar Demonstration at Berthen attended by O.C. Lts Clark & Deane. Lt Douglas (Adj¹) returns from Hospital. O.C. attended conference with the G.O.C. at H.Q. 107th Bde.	
		23	O.C. visited Gun Positions. Generally Quiet.	

109 Brigade R.F.A.

Army Form C. 2118.

WAR DIARY
or
INTELLIGENCE SUMMARY.
(Erase heading not required.)

Instructions regarding War Diaries and Intelligence Summaries are contained in F.S. Regs., Part II. and the Staff Manual respectively. Title pages will be prepared in manuscript.

Place	Date	Hour	Summary of Events and Information	Remarks and references to Appendices
Firing Line	April 24		O.C. visited B.D. & B.A.C. Wagon Lines. Much aeroplane activity. FOKKER machine brought down near PLOEGSTRAAT by A.A. Gun.	
	25		O.C. visited left gone front line trenches with Capt. Hall. Organised bombardment of enemy strong points near KRUISSTRAAT. C.A.F.B. at 3.50 p.m.	
	26		O.C. conducted Capt. Marshall (School of Gunnery) to D/109. Generally quiet on front.	
	27		False gas alarm given on right of Dicm about 2 a.m. Capt. Shaw proceeded on leave. Capt. Gardner to Hospital. G.O.C. R.A. and O.C. visited trenches and O.P.s	
	28		Shoot organised on left gone. Enemy aeroplanes very active all day. Shoot not carried out. Deserter stated attack on left gone probable.	
	29		No enemy activity as expected on left gone. Two deserters stated attack would take place about E1 Trenches tonight or early tomorrow morning.	

109 Brigade R.F.A.

Army Form C. 2118.

WAR DIARY
or
INTELLIGENCE SUMMARY.
(Erase heading not required.)

Instructions regarding War Diaries and Intelligence Summaries are contained in F. S. Regs., Part II. and the Staff Manual respectively. Title pages will be prepared in manuscript.

Place	Date	Hour	Summary of Events and Information	Remarks and references to Appendices
Linghame	Apl. 30th		Enemy commenced bombardment at 1am and followed with gas attack continued until 3 A.M. Gas was not noticable in this area. Wind about 10-16 m.p.h. blowing from due E. Only one communication broken. Gas attack on our left: Div. co-operated with artillery 9-30 p.m. Lt McCullock returned to duty and posted to A/109. 2/Lt Bowder joined Officers Course at BERTHEN.	

H.W.Douglas.
Lieut R.F.A.
for O.C. 109th Brigade R.F.A.

The Officer
    i/c Adjutant Generals Office
        Base.

Herewith Vol.10 of War Diary.

                                            Lt.Col.
31.5.16.   Comdg.109th F.A.B.

109: RAF A
Vol 9
Vol XIV
XXIV

Army Form C. 2118.

WAR DIARY

INTELLIGENCE SUMMARY.
(Erase heading not required.)

Instructions regarding War Diaries and Intelligence Summaries are contained in F.S. Regs., Part II. and the Staff Manual respectively. Title pages will be prepared in manuscript.

Place	Date	Hour	Summary of Events and Information	Remarks and references to Appendices
T23.65	1.5.16		Weather fine. 2nd Lt Darrington joined Brigade. The Brigade has an enfilade fire in position in Ploegsteert Wood, which fires on S.O.S. only.	
	2.5.16		" a little thunder.	
	3.5.16		Lieut. Simpson R.A.M.C. to England. 2nd Lt M Mahon joined Brigade	
	4.5.16		Weather Stormy	
	5.5.16		Lt.Col. Sheffield returned from leave.	
	6.5.16		Lt Clarke Adjt 106th J.A.B. went on leave. 2nd Lt G.M. Ayerbey acting Adjt. Weather fine	
	7.5.16		Weather Stormy. Enemy's artillery remains very quiet.	
	8.5.16		2nd Lieut Darrington went to D.A.C. 2nd Lieut Stroud posted to Brigade.	
	9.5.16		The Brigade fires in conjunction with the heavies in reprisal unto La Petite Douve Farm. Enemy retaliates heavily on Fort his trenches 129 + 130. Weather fine.	
	10.5.16		Major lines C + D Batteries + DAC inspected by Colonel Giller. Draft of 46 Lts. Horses to 6 wheel horses received from D.A.C. also 6 Gunners/ Driver. 2nd Lieut. Hatch joined Brigade. Weather fine.	
	11.5.16			
	12.5.16		Major lines A + B Batteries inspected by Colonel.	
	13.5.16 Noon		Reorganization of Div. Arty. as per GHQ letter No. O.B. 818 28/4/16. – Rainy. Quiet.	
	14.5.16		Brigade Staff on Stopnot Farm.	
	15.5.16			
	16.5.16		Enemy's attitude fairly quiet. Weather improved.	
	17.5.16			

Army Form C. 2118.

VOL X F

WAR DIARY
INTELLIGENCE SUMMARY.
(Erase heading not required.)

Place	Date 1916	Hour	Summary of Events and Information	Remarks and references to Appendices
	18/5		Nothing to Chronicle. [N.a 109th B.H.Q. went into reglet at T.2.3.c.4.2. Instead command of 106th JAB Group. Knife's over to Col. Bruce. 2nd Lieut MacJennings RFA attached to B/109.	
	19/5		— do —	
	20/5		— do — (Battery of 4th Div.)	
	21/5		— do — C.52 took up their A.D. position close to H.Q. with 3 Guns.	
	22/5		Enemy shelled field 200 yards away with 20 15cm H.S. Percussion.	
	23/5		Nothing to Chronicle. Weather some.	
	24/5		Inspection of B & C MG.m lines. Weather improved.	
	25/5		Nothing of note occurred. Weather improved.	
	26/5		Col. Fuller went to turn at H.Q. 108 for a few days	
	27/5		Things very quiet.	
	28/5		— Col. Fuller returned —	
	29/5		Enemy shelled point 2,300 Yards East of H.Q. Obtained direct hit on cottage occupied by a Battery of 41st Div. R.F.A. (who took over from C.52)	
	30/5		Nothing to Chronicle.	
	31/5		"	

O i/c,
   A.G's office
       BASE.

                Herewith War Diary for June 1916.

1/7/16.   *H. Pix Clarke Lieut*
                Adjutant for Lt.Col.
                Comdg. 109th Bde. R.F.A.

109 R.F.A.
V ol 10
Volume XI

Army Form C. 2118.

WAR DIARY
or
INTELLIGENCE SUMMARY.
(Erase heading not required.)

June 1916

Place	Date	Hour	Summary of Events and Information	Remarks and references to Appendices
H.S. T23.c42	16.16		Lieut. H. Pier Clarke return from sick leave. 2/Lt Weatherby to A/106.	
	16.6.16		Nothing to chronicle. Bde. Hd Qrs in rest. Battenie in frank system	
	16.6.16		under other Bde Commanders.	
	17/8/16		night 16/17 gas attack by enemy.	
	17.6.16			
	18.6.16			
	19.16		night 18/19 gas alarm. no fire at Hd. Qrs.	
	20/6/16			
	21.6.16		Draft 2 men to Brigade	
	22.6.16		Capt. J Moore posted to B/109.	
	23.6.16			
	26.6.16			
	26.1.16		2/Lt H Heward to D.A.C. as Capitant.	
	26.1.16		2. Lt Stand to C.C.S.	
	27.6.16			
	28.6.16		night 28/29 Raide on enemy trenches.	
	29.6.16			
	30.1.16			

24/July
Army Form C. 2118.
109 RFA
Volume XII
Vol 11

WAR DIARY or INTELLIGENCE SUMMARY

Place	Date	Hour	Summary of Events and Information	Remarks and references to Appendices
T.23.c.4.2.	1.7.16		Quiet day.	Sheet 28
	2.7.16		Quiet day	
	3.7.16		Considerable Artillery Activity. Had Qrs huh with no shell no casualties	
	4.7.16		In evening Section A/109 and B/109 were relieved by sections of F.A.R aes.	
			2nd AUS. DIV. Section on relief going to wagon line	
	5.7.16		Section B/109 took over wagon line from C/251 at M.35.c.8.4. having marched out in morning	
			Section A/109 marched in evening took up wagon line at M.24.a.5.3 (new lines) Accomodation very scarce ie men area men in bivouacs.	
			After relief at night second section joined first section in new wagon line.	
			1 sec. C/109 relieved by section Rty. 2nd Aus. Div. & went to wagon line.	
			Head Quarters moved to M.18.c.5.2.	
M.18.c.5.2	6.7.16		2nd Section C/109 to Wagon lines	
	7.7.16		1 sec. B/109 relieves 1 sect C/251 Bty at N.34.a.7.2.	
			" 2nd " " "	
			At 4 p.m B/109 came under RIGHT GROUP (H.Qrs WALTHALL & 108 F.A.B. H.Q)	
			A/109 & C/109 were ordered to build new positions	
			B/109 came under LEFT CENTRE GROUP (H.Qrs WALTHALL)	
	9.7.16		In evening C/109 returned to their former position at T.3.0.5.8.	

Army Form C. 2118.

Vol XII

WAR DIARY
or
INTELLIGENCE SUMMARY.
(Erase heading not required.)

Place	Date	Hour	Summary of Events and Information	Remarks and references to Appendices
MBE52			Being parked under Lt Col WALTHALL. Left Combt group.	See Sect 28.
	9/7/16		A/109 marched in morning to former wagon lines & went into action in evening in former position under Lt Col Bone. 106th FAB HQ Right group. A/109 was relieved by 1 Sec C/183 Bty 4th D.A. & this section went into position at T.24.a.2.9. under Lt Col WALTHALL.	
	10/7/16		Nothing to chronicle	
	11/7/16			
	12/7/16		2nd Section A/109 relieved & went to position T.24.a.2.9. At 4pm Battery reprepared A/109 & B/109 in Left group (Lt Col Walthall) C/109 in Centre group (Lt Col Coates)	
	13/7/16		Nothing to chronicle	
	14/7/16		27th Allen & 9th Adair joined, posted & attached to A/109. 1 Sec A/109 withdrawn from action & march to wagon line at M.24.a.5.4. C/106 also withdrawn to M.28.d.2.5. Both Batteries coming under tactical command of C.O. 109 FAB.	
	15/7/16		Work commenced by C/106 & A/109 a position N.22.a.84 & N.16.C.4.0. respectively. Dump of material made in HQ wagon line.	
	16/7/16		Nothing to chronicle	
	17/7/16			
	18/7/16			
	19/7/16			

Army Form C. 2118.

WAR DIARY
or
INTELLIGENCE SUMMARY.
(Erase heading not required.)

Vol XII

Place	Date	Hour	Summary of Events and Information	Remarks and references to Appendices
M.18.c.6	20.7.16		Nothing to Chronicle.	Sheet 57 & 28
	21.7.16	9 am	Hd Qrs marched to P.32.b.6.78 leaving Orderly Officer to hand over. A/109 marched to P.32.b.5.6. In evening remaining section of A/109 came out of action, handing over to B/152.	
P.32.b.56			C/109 & 1 sec B/109 withdrawn from action, marched to P.24.a.6.8. in same Farm.	
	22.7.16		In evening Rem. Sec. B/109 marched to P.24.a.6.3. were relief completed.	
	23.7.16		Nothing to Chronicle.	
	24.7.16		In evening Brigade entrained. Hd Qrs, A/109 at BAILLEUL MAIN A/109 & B/109 at BAILLEUL WEST & B/109 at GODERSWAELDE. In early morning Brigade detrained. B/109 at SALEUX (S.W. of AMIENS) A/109 & C/109 & Hd Qrs at LONGUEAUX (EAST of AMIENS) Batteries marched independently to CROUY where the Brigade was collected. All Rds became in use	
CROUY	26.7.16			

Army Form C. 2118.

WAR DIARY
or
~~INTELLIGENCE SUMMARY.~~
(Erase heading not required.)

Vol XII

Place	Date	Hour	Summary of Events and Information	Remarks and references to Appendices
CROUY	27.7.16		Brigade Training.	
	28.7.16		Brigade Training. Capt. T.F. Donworth accidentally drowned	
	29.7.16		" "	
	30.7.16		" "	
DAOURS	31.7.16		Brigade marched to DAOURS starting at 2.45pm + arriving about 10.0pm. Brigade Divisional Artillery all billeted together close to river, now in bivouacs.	

24th Divisional Artillery

109th BRIGADE

ROYAL FIELD ARTILLERY

AUGUST 1 9 1 6

SECRET.

Headquarters,
    24th Divisional Artillery.   Vol 12

Herewith Vol XIII of War Diary.

H Pier Clarke Lieut
    a/for   Lt.Col.
6.9.16.   Commanding 109th F.A.B.

Army Form C. 2118.

VOL XIII

WAR DIARY
or
INTELLIGENCE SUMMARY.
(Erase heading not required.)

Place	Date	Hour	Summary of Events and Information	Remarks and references to Appendices
1-8-16 DAOURS	1.8.16		Training. East Barton Ave. arrived attached A/154	
	2.8.16		Training	
	3.8.16		Training	
	4.8.16		Brigade marched to BOIS DES TAILLES starting at 8.30 am. B. Battery leading followed by C. & A. Brigade in bivouac with few tents.	
BOIS DES TAILLES	5.8.16		In Camp	
	6.8.16		Brigade ordered to build three positions in valley S.22.a Central Sheet 57.C. Cover was made in form of trenches but no actual gun pits were dug	
	7.8.16		No work done on account of tactical operations.	
	8.8.16		More work done on positions.	
	9.8.16		C.O. & Battery Commanders reconnoitred new position in square A.10.a	
	10.8.16		Sheet 62.C. Mr Bell & attached to 'A' Battery	
	11.8.16		Work done on positions in Square A.10.a (sheet 62c) Colonel Cuney & orderly officer proceed to Hd Qrs 158 Bde near OXFORD COPSE to reconnoitre.	

WAR DIARY
or
INTELLIGENCE SUMMARY.

VOL XIII

Place	Date	Hour	Summary of Events and Information	Remarks and references to Appendices
A.15.c.4.5	12.8.16	8 am	109th Brigade takes over from 158 Bde at Hdqrs A.15.c.4.5 (sheet 62c). Bde moved to new wagon lines at 1h noon in E.24.a (sheet 62d). Bde ordered to fire to as attached order. (1) Casualties 3 O.R.	
	13.8.16		Weather during morning as order (II) Casualties nil.	
	14.8.16		Fairly quiet day. Btys fired on back area. Casualties nil.	
	15.8.16		Remaining time out as in order (III) Casualties 1 O.R.	
	16.8.16		Preliminary operation order (IV) Draft of 10 gunners to R.B.Ey. Casualties 3 O.R.	
	17.8.16		Attack on Stong Point as order (V) Casualties 4 O.R.	
	18.8.16		Attack on GUILLEMONT Casualties 10th 2 O.R. (21st R.C DACIE)	Appendix I.
	19.8.16		At 7 am attached to 3° DA for tactical administration.	
	20.8.16		Operation against STRONG POINT as order	
	21.8.16		Fairly quiet day. B.Cs registered. Aeroplane brought down. Pilot killed & wounded.	
	22.8.16		Artillery of both sides active.	
	23.8.16		Quiet day.	
	24.8.16		Quiet day.	
	25.8.16		Brigade moved to position in valley N. of MONTAUBAN. Map Ref: Hd Qrs S.22.d.9.2. A.Bty S.22.d.6.9. B.Bty S.22.c.7.3. C.Bty S.22.a.5.7. Casualties 3 wounded 1 killed.	
	26.8.16		Registered on Sunken Road in front ARROW HEAD copse	

Army Form C. 2118.

VOL XIII

WAR DIARY
or
INTELLIGENCE SUMMARY.

(Erase heading not required.)

Instructions regarding War Diaries and Intelligence Summaries are contained in F. S. Regs., Part II. and the Staff Manual respectively. Title pages will be prepared in manuscript.

Place	Date	Hour	Summary of Events and Information	Remarks and references to Appendices
S.22.c.9.2.	27/8/16		Operations against GUILLEMONT commenced but were postponed on account of bad weather.	
	28/8/16		Bad weather. 1 killed 3 wounded.	
	29/8/16		Bombardment again ordered but cancelled on account of weather.	
	30/8/16		Quiet day.	
	31/8/16		Capt GOODWIN killed. O.R. Ranks total of 8 killed 9 wounded 2 missing. Heavy bombardment by enemy all day.	

APPENDIX 1

Orders stating that the 24th Division would attack GUILLEMONT were received about 10.0.a.m.,18.8.16.

Battery Commanders had previously registered points on the Brigade front, from front line.

Signalling & Liaison Arrangements were as follows :-
2 F.O.O's, 2/Lt.Dale & 2/Lt.Addington "B" Battery were detailed with party consisting of signallers and runners to go to Btn.H.Q.of 13th Middlesex Regt. near which was No.4 Visual Signalling Station,(S.30.c.5.3.)

No.3 Station, in communication by visual with No.4, was established at A.11.a.8.2.

No.2 Station was a central station at "B" Battery in communication with No.3 by telephone and with Bde.H.Q.and Batteries by Visual and telephone.

No.1 Station at Bde.H.Q.,Telephone and Visual.

Until about 5.0.p.m. this worked very well until No.4 Station was knocked out by a direct hit and 2/Lt.DALE killed.

Continual reports were being received that an 18-pdr Battery was shooting short on ARROW HEAD COPSE, consequently from 1.10.p.m. - 1.30.p.m. the C.O. checked the lines of the Batteries by observing salvoes from Hd.Qrs.

This checking and the fact that the Battery Commanders had each registered from the front line practically eliminated any possibility of any Battery of the Brigade being the one which was shooting short, especially as Brigade lines of fire went to Right (i.e., South) of ARROW HEAD COPSE.

During the course of the morning "A" Battery had a gun put out of action on account of piston trouble. This gun was taken out and sent to workshops during afternoon.

ZERO TIME was 2.45.p.m. and programme was carried out.

The Brigade Barrage as observed from Brigade H.Q. appeared good.

At 3.35.p.m. a message from F.O.O. was received as follows (begins) SEAL, Drop Artillery fire back onto strong point on Right, F.O.O.,KITTY.

At 3.40.p.m. visual message picked up as follows (begins) BRANCH, Our left company gained objective helped by Support Company AAA Right still held up KITTY (ends)

Two more messages were received from F.O.O. saying Artillery were shooting short at S.30.d.3.9. to S.30.d.3.3.

About 5.0.p.m. No.23442 Corporal Ross and No 23335 Gunner Haggarty arrive at "B" Battery from Btn.H.Q., with message saying that No.4 Visual Station had been knocked out by direct hit, that 2/Lieut.DALE had been killed, and that 2/Lieut ADDINGTON was at Btn.H.Q. with two men remaining of the party.

It was impossible for runners to get to No.3 Station across the MALTZ HORN VALLEY.

"B" Battery had a gun out of action from 5.0.p.m. to 7.0.p.m. put right by Armament Artificer.

At 8.55.p.m. new barrage was ordered by 24th D.A.
"A" Battery   T.25.a.5½.2½. - T.25.a.5½.8½.
"B & C" Batteries S.30.b.9½.8. - T.25.a.5½.8½.

At 9.20.p.m. following received from D.A.
"Do not shoot West of T.25.a.2½.7½."

9.50.p.m., "A" Battery & "B" Battery put on to barrage T.25.a.5½.2½. to T.25.a.5½.8½., "C" Battery T.25.a.3.8.-T.25.a.5½.8½ A slow rate of fire was kept up on this barrage all night.

At midnight orders received saying that programme for 19th was cancelled.

Difficulty was experienced in the supply of ammunition as the advanced Refilling Point was empty for a considerable period on evening and night of 18th and 18th/19th

APPENDIX 1. (cont)

Amount of ammunition on hand 5.0.a.m.,19th
"A" Battery 2,000 rounds
             500 rounds a gun
             of which 1,300 was H.E.
"B" Battery 718 rounds
             179 rounds a gun
At this time Battery received 7 wagons making total of
             1,250 rounds
             312 rounds a gun
"C" Battery 930 rounds
             232 rounds a gun
and 600 rounds on the way up to position makes
             1,530 rounds
             382 rounds a gun.
Batteries being considerably below establishment of 800 rounds a gun.

Os.C.
Batteries.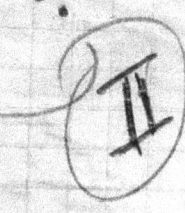

Reference attached,
The registrations for to-morrow are cancelled.
Batteries will cut wire on the front line allotted to the Brigade commencing at once, as follows :-

A/109 T.25.b.1.5. to road T.25.a.7.4. inclusive
B/109 Road T.25.a.7.4. to point T.25.a.3.4. inclusive
C/109 T.25.a.3.4. to S.30.b.9½.7.

Times for cutting will be notified to-night by wire.
Attached orders and map to be initalled passed, and returned   To reach:-
A Battery by 10.p.m.
B   :   11.p.m.
C   :   12.midnight.

                                H Pier Clarke   Lieut.
13.8.16.   Adjutant 109th F.A.B?

A   AL. 10.15 p.m.
B   10.20 p.m.
C   PYD. 11.0 p.m.

Os.C.
    Batteries.

        The remaining wire to be cut is
T.25.b.7.4. to T.25.a.2.2.
A/109 will cut 100 yards on each side
of points T.25.A.2.2.and T.25.B.0.4.
i.e. the points where the trenches join.
B/109 will cut from T.25.A.2.2.to Road
T.25.A.7.7.Inclusive.
C/109 will cut Road T.25.A.7.7. to
T.25.B.0.4. Inclusive.
        This will be carried out to-day
and to-night from previous registrations.
        Back areas allotted must not be
neglected.

                                    Lieut.
15.8.16.   Adjutant 109th F.A.B.

Reference 57.C.S.W.

Programme for Shoot 16/8/16.

(IV)

1st Phase

Objective.
"A" Battery T.25.c.3.8. to T.25.c.1.8½.
"B"   ;   T.25.c.1.8½ to S.30.b.9.0.
"C"   ;   S.30.b.9.0. to S.30.b.7.0.

Rate of Fire
5.10 - 30 mins to - 15 mins   Ordinary   5.25
5.25 - 15 ;   ; - 3 ;   Medium   5.37
5.37 - 3   ;   ; + 3 ;   Intense   5.43

2nd Phase.

5.43 + 3 mins   Lift 50 yards from objective in
                first phase.
5.44 + 4 ;   Lift again 50 yards and continue
                to lift 50 yards every minute
                till on line.

A Battery T.25.b.1.4. to T.25.a.7.6.
B   ;   T.25.a.7.6. to T.25.a.3.7.
C   ;   T.25.a.3.7. to T.25.a.0.9.

Rate of Fire
+ 3 mins to   30 mins   Intense
+ 30   ;   1 hour   Medium
+ 1 hour ;   2 hours   Ordinary
+ 2 hours ;   till stopped   1 round per
                             Battery per min.

Please report by wire No. of lifts from first objective to second.

Issued at 5.5.a.m.

16.8.16.   Lieut.
                        Adjutant 109th F.A.B.

SECRET   BM 550

106th F.A.B.
107th " " "
108th " " "
109th " " "
2nd D.A.
T.M., 24th D.A.

Reference 24th D.A. Order No.4.

"ZERO" hour on the 16th August will be 5-40.p.m.

This time will be communicated only to those immediately concerned, and is on no account to be communicated by telephone.

Please acknowledge.

16/8/16.   Captain.R.A.

Brigade Major, 24th Divisional Artillery.

Os.C.

    Batteries.

Reference attached order
Zones will be as follows :-
    C/109 S.30.b.9.½. to T.25.c.½.9.
A/109 & B/109 T.25.c.½.9. to T.25.c.3.8.

    The 72nd Brigade are <u>attacking</u> and
<u>consolidating</u> strong point S.30.b.6.2.

    Accuracy for line is essential
especially by C/109 on account of close
shooting.

                                    Lieut.
17.5.6.   Adjutant 109th F.A.B.

SECRET

O's.C.
   Batteries.

Batteries will fire to-night on Zones T.25.c.3.6. to 8.30.b.9.½.

Shrapnel will be used.

Rate of Fire

   Zero + 10 minutes Intense.
   + 10   : to + 20 mins. Medium
   + 20   : to + 1 hour Ordinary
   + 1 hour till stopped Slow.
       i.e. 1 round per Bty. per minute.

Zero is at 10.p.m.

Previous orders for shoot at this hour are cancelled.

                                Lieut.
17.3.16.   Adjutant 109th F.A.B.

O.C. Batteries.

1. The 20th Divn will attack on afternoon August 30th in conjunction with 6th Divn on right & 7th Divn on left.

2. Final objective of 20th Divn is WEDGE WOOD — Givenchy road from T.26.a.18 — T.20.a.15½.

3. There will be a preliminary bombardment by Heavy Arty. 46 Hours with lulls for Chinese attacks.

Bombardment will commence at steady rate 8am 29th & continue at steady rate till zero — 1 hr 35 min on 30th from which hour it will gradually increase in rate up to zero — 40 min at which hour it will become intense remaining so till zero hour.

4. All ranks must be aware of the great importance of this operation.
It has got to succeed.

Artillery programme as far as is known at present.

29th Slow deliberate fire except where otherwise stated.

8am - 2·5pm Bombardment & registration.

2·5pm - 2·7pm Front & support trenches in Bde. areas. 3 rounds rapid fire.

2·7pm - 6·30pm Bombardment.

Night 29th/30th Usual night firing

30th 8am - 10·15am Bombardment.

10·15am Front support and communication trenches in Bde areas. 3 rounds rapid fire

10·15am - 11·30am Bombardment.

11.30 am – 11.35 am   Intense fire on
                Area T.19.d.4.5. –
                T.20.c.1.6. – T.19.d.4.9.

11.35 am to – 1 hr 35 min Bombardment.

– 1 hr 35 min to – 40 min Ground
           likely to contain machine
           guns in Bde Areas. To
           fire occasional bursts.

Remainder of programme follows

later.

28.8.16   H Pras Clarke Lieut
                  Adjutant 109 PA Bde

SECRET.

O.C. Battery

Continuation of Artillery programme

−40 mins to zero Bombardment.

Zero to +2 mins S.30 b.7.2 − S.30 b.8.7.
Lift 50 yards at +2 min &
continue lifting 50 yards every
minute till on next barrage.

+7 min. to +10 min T.25.a 3/2.3 to T.25.a 2.7
Lift 50 yards at +10 min &
continue lifting 50 yards every
minute till on next barrage.

+13 min to +60 min T.25.a 7.4 to T.25.a 6.8.
Lift 100 yards at +60 min &
continue lifting 100 yards every
4 min till on next barrage.

+67 min to +120 min T.25.b.5.6½ to T.19.d.5.0
Lift 50 yards at +120 min &
continue lifting 50 yards every
min till on next barrage.

+130 min till stopped T.26.a 5.7½ to
T.20.c.5/2.1.

Rates of Fire.

Zero to +15 min.   Intense
+15 min to +50 min   Ordinary
+50 min to +65 min   Intense
+65 min to +120 min   Ordinary
+120 min to +145 min   Intense
+145 till stopped   Ordinary.

———

Please note that there may be alterations in this programme.

28.8.16   H. Piers Clarke Lieut
            Adjutant 109 F A Bde

O.C. Batteries:

① For the attack tomorrow the 109th Brigade cover part of front of 59th Inf. Bde whose objectives are as follows:-

(a) German trenches in Sunken Road from T.25.a.3½.3 to T.25.a.2.7½; thence north to ~~Mount Street~~ MOUNT STREET.

(b) Trench Junction T.25.b.1.4½ (incl.) thence SOUTH STREET as far as MOUNT STREET

(c) WEDGE WOOD – GINCHY road from T.26.a.1.7 to Cross roads T.20.c.1½.4½

② Advance from (a) to (b) will commence at 0+50 min.

Advance from (b) to c will commence at 0+2 hours

③ A "pusher" mine under the strong point at S.30.c.6.7.2 will be exploded at zero minus 10 secs and the

Flammenwerfer will open fire at the same time if in position.

Assaulting troops of 59th + 60th Inf Bdes will carry RED and Yellow flags respectively.

29816 H Pris Clarke Lieut
Adjutant 109 Bde

www.ingramcontent.com/pod-product-compliance
Lightning Source LLC
Chambersburg PA
CBHW081548160426
43191CB00011B/1865